Head & Heart

Helen Flanagan
Head & Heart

MIRROR BOOKS

MIRROR BOOKS

Content Warning: This book contains themes of mental illness, eating disorders, self harm and suicide.

Copyright © Helen Flanagan

The right of Helen Flanagan to be identified as the owner of this work has been asserted in accordance with the Copyright, Designs and Patents Act, 1988. All Rights Reserved.

No part of this publication may be reproduced, stored in a retrieval system, or transmitted in any form, or by any means, electronic, mechanical, photocopying, recording or otherwise without the prior permission in writing of the copyright holders, nor be otherwise circulated in any form of binding or cover other than in which it is published and without a similar condition being imposed on the subsequent publisher.

Written with Beth Neil

1

First published in hardback in Great Britain and Ireland in 2026 by Mirror Books, a Reach PLC business.

www.mirrorbooks.co.uk
@TheMirrorBooks

ISBN: 9781917439633
eBook ISBN: 9781917439640

Photographic acknowledgements:
Alamy, MirrorPix, Helen Flanagan Personal Collection

Every effort has been made to trace copyright. Any oversights will be rectified in future editions.

Editing and Production: Christine Costello, Lawrence Matheson
Cover Design: Chris Collins

Printed and bound by CPI Group (UK) Ltd, Croydon, CR0 4YY.

For Matilda, Delilah and Charlie.
My world.

Contents

Author's Note	9
Prologue	13
Early Signs	15
Streets Ahead	29
Off the Rails	52
Spiralling	72
Freedom	87
Get Me Out of Here	101
Intrusions	124
New Beginnings	150
Periods of Hell	169
Beginning of the End	184
Single Life	208
Love Struck	224
The Unravelling	240
Recovery	260
Court Out	273
Facing the Future	284
One Last Thing…	295
Acknowledgements	299

Author's Note

HI, FRIENDS…

First of all, I'd like to thank you for being here. It means more to me than you probably realise.

Sitting down to write about my life and all its ups and downs was a daunting task because I knew if I was going to do it justice, it would mean laying everything out there.

I was going to have to revisit painful times, digging deep into experiences I'd have much rather left buried in the past.

But telling my truth meant no hiding – no glossing over or airbrushing.

I don't think I've done anything particularly extraordinary over the years, I've never claimed to be anyone special. But as a woman and a mother of three and someone who has loved, lost, battled back from the brink and always tried her best to keep going, I hope there is something about me that people can relate to.

So many of us live in the space between holding it together and falling apart and that can often feel like a lonely place.

I've made mistakes, I've been hurt and I've had to rebuild from rock bottom, but I've also learned, grown and come out the other side a stronger, better person.

Some of you will already know that the start of 2024 was catastrophic for me after an episode of severe psychosis triggered by a reaction to my ADHD medication left me broken and with everything good in my life hanging in the balance.

My recovery took time and an enormous amount of strength as well as the support of the people around me. Not to mention the endless love I have for my three children who gave me all the motivation I needed to get well again.

They are, and always will be, my reason.

But the truth is, I've struggled with my mental health for years and thanks to the knowledge and awareness I have now, I know the roots started to take hold in early childhood, even before I joined the cast of *Coronation Street* at the age of nine.

As a kid, I knew something felt different. Wrong, sometimes.

The anxiety, obsessive thoughts and spirals of emotion which I couldn't explain or control… they were there all along, I just didn't have the words for any of it. It's taken literally decades to unpick everything, to truly understand what makes me tick and to learn how to be kinder to myself.

Writing about all this is something I've wanted to do

for a while; it's been like a burning need to use my experience and platform. Motherhood, relationships and mental health are the threads that are woven through every part of my life, each one crossing over with and complicating the others – I wanted to explore all of that, but my head was never in quite the right place to get started. Either I wasn't ready, or I was still in the thick of it and my ADHD makes it hard to focus and concentrate even at the best of times.

So it's been a case of waiting for the right moment.

And I'm not writing now because I've figured it all out (I definitely haven't!), it's more about coming to the realisation that maybe sharing the chaos just as it is – raw and unfinished – is exactly what someone else might need to read.

I know all of that sounds pretty heavy and parts of this book absolutely are because I've not shied away from it. But it's certainly not all doom and gloom! Yes, there's pain and heartbreak, but I've always used humour as a survival tool and there are plenty of stories in here that will make you smile and perhaps even give you some LOLZ.

A quick disclaimer, though. I'm not a medical expert and despite the shedload of therapy I've had over the years, I don't have all the answers, nor will I pretend to. In short, this book isn't going to offer any clinical advice. If you're struggling, please seek the help of a professional who can help you because you deserve care and safety.

I'm a big believer in the power of shared experience and the healing that can come from hearing someone say, 'Babe, me too.'

I've drawn on so many brave voices in the past and now I want to add mine to the mix. I don't think I've been through more than anyone else and no doubt I've got a load more shit to go through yet, but if this book helps even one person feel seen or understood, then it's been worth it.

So here we go. This is my story, messy and unfiltered. And it's offered to you with an open heart in the hope that somewhere between these lines, you might find something you need.

Prologue

January 9th 2024

I HAVEN'T SLEPT. HOW CAN I sleep when someone is trying to kill me?

How can I rest when I'm being watched, filmed, hunted down, possibly even drugged?

The house isn't safe – I don't care what the police said last night when they came round responding to my desperate 999 call. I know for a fact there were men outside and they were trying to break in to get me.

I can't believe it's taken me so long to work this out, but it all makes sense now. I see it so clearly and I know my life is in danger.

I go downstairs and check the locks again. My jaw is clenched, my whole body tense, my mind racing. I have to stay on high alert – the second I let my guard down, they'll pounce and it'll be game over.

I can't trust anyone, they're probably all in on it. Everything feels like a threat and it's building towards something dreadful so I need to stay one step ahead.

FFS. I have to get the children ready for school, we're already massively late. I'm wired and running only on adrenaline while trying to butter toast, pour out cereal, fill up water bottles and find three pairs of shoes.

Why can I never find their shoes?!

My brain is screaming that something horrific is about to happen, but I can't let the children know anything is amiss, so I fix a smile as if nothing is wrong. I don't think they are any the wiser.

But those bastards outside are watching. Waiting.

And I have no idea if I'm going to make it through the day alive.

Chapter One

Early Signs

I CAN PINPOINT ALMOST THE exact moment when everything shifted. The juncture where something in me changed, as if a switch had flicked inside my head, a switch I'm pretty sure has never flicked back.

It came halfway through Year Four at St John's Primary School in Bolton when I was eight years old and had a falling out with my two best friends, Beth and Laura. The three of us had formed a little girlband called Silver Rain (I know, LOL) and every breaktime we'd practise performing some totally cringe song I'd written that morning, perfecting the dance routines and thinking we were *definitely* going to be the next Spice Girls.

Even bigger than them, actually.

Until one day Laura pulled a proper Geri Halliwell and told me and Beth that she didn't want to be in the group anymore. I think she maybe wanted to focus on her skipping technique instead so let's call it 'artistic differences'.

I was completely heartbroken about the prospect of the band breaking up just when we were on the verge of stardom and pleaded with Laura to change her mind, but she'd made her decision and there was no going back. So my heartbreak turned to anger and I was so cross that, in a fit of pure petulance, I told Laura I was going to write to *Girl Talk* magazine about her so everyone would know exactly what she'd done. That'd show her.

I mean, clearly I needed to chill, but it was just a stupid quarrel between friends, the kind that goes on in playgrounds up and down the country every single day and which always blows over as quickly as it blew up.

Only this one didn't.

The next day Laura wasn't in school – she'd refused to come in, too upset because of what had happened – and I was summoned to the head's office where I was shouted at for being a bully.

For a goody two-shoes like me who always followed the rules, was never in trouble and had certainly not been yelled at like that before, the whole episode was a distressing experience. Obviously I felt awful for Laura and totally regretted threatening to write to *Girl Talk* about her hand in Silver Rain's break-up, but to stand accused of 'bullying' her was gut-wrenching to me and also seemed incredibly unfair.

I knew I wasn't a bully.

I was just a kid who had slightly overreacted to a run-of-the-mill spat, but the backlash felt shocking and disproportionate. And it affected me so badly that from that day, I started to feel panicky about going to school, anxious that everyone thought I was a nasty piece of work and that I was going to get shouted at again.

I went into myself, forming an imaginary protective shell around me and became nervous about speaking up in class. I developed an obsession over who wasn't in school each day and whether their absence was because they thought I'd been bullying them too.

It wasn't just a rude awakening to the fact that not everything in life is hunky-dory and that sometimes there are going to be bumps in the road, but it also seemed to lay the foundations for a series of psychological reactions which, in hindsight, I've been battling ever since.

I've often wondered whether everything that came next might have unfolded differently had the situation been handled more sensitively all round.

And I know it probably seems so insignificant and nothing beyond the normal shenanigans of day-to-day school life, but even thinking about it now all these years later triggers something and I find myself crying.

I've also no doubt that most other kids would have managed to get over the whole thing quite quickly, formed Silver Rain 2.0 with a replacement member just like the Sugababes. But I was never 'most other kids' and I couldn't get past it.

Up until then, everything about my childhood had been so... *nice*. Achingly ordinary, in fact. I was a very confident little girl, bright, bubbly and outgoing, which I think came from the security of my home life and the love my mum and dad had enveloped me in. I'd always felt very safe and my parents were dead soft with me – I wasn't ever a naughty child so I never gave them much to worry about.

My, ahem, rebellious phase came later, coinciding with the arrival of a 10-ton truck of hormones. Hold tight and I'll tell you all about that in due course...

I was born Helen Joyce Flanagan on August 7th 1990 at The Royal Bolton Hospital – my middle name was after my dad's mum who passed away from cancer when he was in his early 20s and it's always felt like a real privilege to carry that as a tribute to her.

She grew up in the village I live in today and went to the same school my three children go to, which feels like a beautiful full circle moment. Nana Joyce is even buried in the grounds of the church opposite my house and knowing she's there always makes me feel quite protected in a funny kind of way.

I'm the third child of four – my older siblings Jane and Tom were nine and 10 when I was born so there was quite a gap between us – and my little sister Jessica came along two years after me, making us a happy, tight-knit family of six.

My mum and dad, Julia and Paul, have been together

since they were about 19 which I think is really cute! They were just 21 when they married and have always had a lovely relationship – even now my dad will give my mum an affectionate tap on the bum which, of course, makes me feel ILL because they're my parents, but it is actually dead sweet. He's obsessed with her and I can honestly say I've never seen Mum and Dad argue.

The only time they came close to falling out was when we'd go on our annual family holiday to Eurocamp in France and Mum would make a mess of trying to read the map while Dad drove our Peugeot down to Portsmouth to catch the ferry.

She's a fantastic mother (and has since proved an equally fantastic grandmother), but her navigation skills left a lot to be desired. Sorry, Mum!

She'd make us four kids a 'lucky bag' each for those long car journeys, filled with magazines, notebooks, pens, puzzle books and crafts and we all found the mystery around what was in them so exciting!

I guess we were what you might call a traditional, working-class family – my dad went out to work and gave my mum the budget to run the house. Dad's an electrician by trade and worked long hours in the family business alongside his father, Joe, which meant he'd leave the house at quarter to five every morning while we were all still sleeping – we wouldn't see him until he came home at teatime.

I used to look forward to hearing his key in the lock

every evening and my memories of that excitement are so clear that I can still feel the tingles now… funny what stays with you, isn't it?

Mum worked here and there – she had jobs as a classroom assistant and a childminder – but she mostly stayed at home, running the household and looking after us kids, which, I know now is one of the hardest jobs in the world. You *really* don't appreciate that until you become a mum yourself.

My grandad Joe (Dad's dad) lived nearby with his second wife, a lovely lady called Liz. And my mum's parents – Nana Nancy and Grandad Guy – were also a big part of our lives. They lived in the Lake District, on the farm where Mum grew up, and Nancy was a proper Nana, if that makes sense. She was everything you'd imagine a Nana to be with her cuddles, kisses and cooking – her baking was amazing; she used to make this chocolate flake cake which was to die for.

My grandad passed away when I was about 10, but we were lucky enough to have Nana until 2022 and she was a super classy lady right to the end, elegant and well-spoken and just totally gorgeous. I adored her.

I was surrounded by lots of family who loved me. From what I've learned since, money was always fairly tight – after all it's not cheap raising four children on a single income – but my parents shielded us from any financial concerns and I certainly didn't want for anything, growing up in the semi-detached, four-bed family home in Bolton which Mum and Dad still live in today.

I shared a bedroom with Jessica which had bunk beds with matching bed sets from the Next catalogue and was decorated with pink heart wallpaper. I was much more 'girly' than Jessica, always into mothering my dolls and from a young age I loved flipping through the shopping catalogue, picking out baby clothes for my future children to wear. That strong maternal instinct has been there throughout my life and it's why I had my kids relatively young – I was 24 when my eldest Matilda was born in 2015.

Fashion was a big thing for me from early on and my favourite thing to do on a Saturday was to take a trip to Tammy Girl in Bolton with my mum, a clothes heaven where I'd be in my element. I was also obsessed with all the Disney princesses and actually wanted to be Belle, from *Beauty and the Beast* who I'd dress up as, parading around the house in my swishy, yellow gown. Both Jessica and I were into Disney movies far more than we were into television programmes and we watched *The Little Mermaid* so many times I could probably still recite the entire script from start to finish.

My mum has told me that when I started primary school, I was a proper nightmare to settle, mainly due to the fact I wasn't allowed to wear my prized plastic tiara from the Disney Store – an essential item as far as my four-year-old self was concerned.

One of my earliest memories is of my older sister Jane putting my hair in a French plait before school. She was a moody teenager by this time who fully resented having to do this and made her disgruntlement only too clear, shoving me aggressively into position, gripping my head between her knees and then tugging at my hair really roughly to get the plait in. On each side of my face, I could feel the prickles on her legs from where she'd shaved them.

Because of the gap between me, Jane and Tom, I was always closest to Jessica and we shared everything as kids, although we are chalk and cheese as people. Jessica was much more academic than me, flying through school and uni and today she's really settled as a mum-of-two with her fiancé in one of the best, most loving and stable relationships I know.

I remember being jealous of her naturally white-blonde hair – mine was boring old mousey brown and I've seen artwork my mum has kept where I've drawn myself in a beautiful pink dress with long, flowing blonde locks and a crown perched on my head and Jessica as a half-hearted scribble with messy black hair and a horrible brown dress – how hilarious is that?!

As the eldest of the two, I tended to be 'in charge' and before school we'd put on shows for Mum where I always cast myself as the star as well as both the choreographer and director, giving Jessica a tiny token part so she wouldn't steal my thunder. Honestly, what was

I like? There was a lot of main character energy, put it that way.

Funnily enough, Jessica ended up auditioning for the role of my on-screen *Coronation Street* sister Sophie, losing out to Brooke Vincent, so in another life we could have starred on the show together. But she was never into drama anything like as much as me – she attended the same theatre group but could always take it or leave it and she wasn't ever envious of the work that I went on to do.

I fell head over heels in love with performing at the age of about six, and it was thanks mainly to my mum who is brilliant at recognising kids' strengths and then finding outlets for those talents and interests – she recently got my second daughter Delilah into a football team where she's absolutely thriving.

She found Carol Godby's drama group over in Bury, about half an hour away from where we lived, which has long been a real breeding ground for young actors in the north west – loads of the kids from *Corrie* and *Emmerdale* have been plucked from Carol's over the years. In fact, my daughter Matilda goes there now so watch this space!

It wasn't long before I started to get auditions and calls to castings in London and I was soon doing commercials for the likes of Fairy Liquid and Adams clothing which was thrilling for a young girl like me coming from an ordinary family in Bolton.

My mum never put any pressure on me and would

only say before an audition, 'Just go in there and be your lovely self' which gave me the belief that I could do it. Although me and Mum clashed a bit during my teens, back then I was very much a mummy's girl.

I think it was when I appeared in my first pantomime for Carol Godby where I played a pink fairy called Sugar Dummy that I knew this was what I wanted to do forever. I loved being on stage and, to be completely honest, I revelled in being the centre of attention. Some things never change, eh?

So outside of the classroom I'd found my passion, discovering a joy in performing which would take me on the most exciting and unpredictable of journeys. But in school I remained deeply unhappy.

Not long after the bullying accusations, I started to experience horrible, torturous and recurrent thoughts which made me question whether I was really my mum and dad's child. I became fixated on the idea that I was actually my older sister's daughter – in my bizarre little mind, she was my real mum and the people I called Mum and Dad were really my grandparents who had taken me on as their own to cover up Jane's pregnancy.

It sounds so ridiculous now, but these persistent thoughts became a complete preoccupation, that I couldn't shake and I'd set about finding evidence, however flimsy, to fit my theory. I pinned a lot on me and Jane looking very similar, and so therefore she must be my mother.

These were the very early signs of what I now know to be Obsessive Compulsive Disorder, a mental health condition characterised by unwanted, intrusive thoughts which can send you crackers – some of them seriously dark.

Although I want to be as honest as I can here and I'm going to be talking a lot more about how devastating this condition has been for me personally, a lot of my OCD-driven thoughts are far too disturbing to share publicly. It's a terrible, scary place to be and very isolating too because it feels impossible to tell anyone what's going on inside your head – it's too shameful to say out loud and you think there's no way anyone would understand.

The saddest, sickest points of my life have been as a result of OCD and there have been times when I've felt like I was literally going mad. The older I've got, the more grotesque and out of control my thoughts have become and although I know I am not my thoughts – the OCD is *not* me – they feel completely real.

Rationale goes out the window.

I've no idea where most of them come from, sometimes it's like, 'Fucking hell, what was *that* all about?!' but this is an illness which preys on you and shows no mercy.

As a kid, I'd see things on the news and stew over them for days. I became focused on the cellar in our house and what was down there, torturing myself with thoughts of kidnap victims or dead bodies.

When I went to my swimming lessons, I'd convince

myself I was actually in the ocean and there were sharks circling in the water and become overwhelmed with panic. It was all so graphic and lifelike to me and there was nothing I could do to get these thoughts out of my brain. I was trapped.

Weirdly, Matilda has the exact same thoughts about sharks in the water and now refuses to go to swimming lessons. Sometimes in the middle of the night she'll wake me up to tell me that she feels like she's in the sea and surrounded by sharks and I absolutely know what she's going through – it's like history repeating itself.

'Darling,' I'll say, 'sometimes your brain tells you silly things and plays tricks on you. I promise you it's not real.'

Some of the worst of these intrusive thoughts would happen in church of all places and that started when I was about nine. As a committed Catholic family, my parents would make us attend Mass every Saturday night and because I was into drama, my dad volunteered me to be an altar girl which meant I had to do a reading each week. He was coming from a good place – he was so proud of me and I didn't want to let him down – but in the days beforehand, I'd get intrusive thoughts about (and there's no delicate way to put this, I'm afraid) shitting myself in front of the whole church. The more I thought about it, the more certain I was that it was going to happen.

The build-up to the service would be agony as these thoughts swirled around my head and I'd picture it happening right there in front of the kids from school, the whole congregation and all my parents' friends. Everyone would see, and it would be the worst thing in the world.

When it came to the point I had to stand up and read, I'd race through my words as quickly as I could, not daring to look up even once and then as soon as it was over, I'd dash to the toilet to check that I hadn't actually soiled myself. Which, by the way, I never had, but the images in my mind felt so very real and I had to stop going to church because it became such a trigger point.

I was lucky that I had the kind of relationship with my mum where I could open up and I did find the courage to share some of what was going on with her. I recall talking to her while she was shaving her legs in the bath one evening and I was worried she'd think I was a total freak, but to my surprise, she listened and understood, recognising a lot of herself in what I was describing.

Maybe it's hereditary because I also spoke to my nana Nancy before she passed away and discovered that she too had struggled with bouts of depression and hormonal imbalances her whole life. To me, my nana was always this very strong woman – farmers' wives have to be – so that was a real eye-opener and proof that you can never really know what anyone's internal struggles are if they are determined to keep them well hidden.

Making life even more challenging was that in school things were going from bad to worse. My anxieties meant I'd effectively isolated myself and that made me an easy target to be picked on; there was one girl in particular who was vicious to me daily and I was completely terrified of her. I was a sensitive, soft-natured kid with no clue about how to stick up for myself and she spotted this 'weakness' and exploited it.

She'd steal my pens, make fun of the way I looked and say nasty, humiliating things to me in return for laughs from the others and I had to hide from her in the playground breaktime to avoid another attack.

I had come to hate having to go into school. Every day was exhausting, having to keep my head down and make myself small to minimise the risk of being crucified.

Drama, therefore, took on an even greater significance for me and became something of a salvation. It was a safe space, a refuge from the daily grind. At school I was an outsider, but over at Carol Godby's I was accepted and included, and it was somewhere I could be totally myself; I didn't have to hide away.

And it was through my love of performance that I found an escape. Because I was about to have an audition which would change the course of my whole life.

Chapter Two

Streets Ahead

EVERY SO OFTEN I GET asked what I'd be doing if I hadn't been on *Coronation Street*. It's something I've given a fair bit of thought to over the years, but I always come back to the same answer: fuck knows.

It's difficult to put into words how much of a big deal it was, landing the part of Rosie Webster and joining this Great British institution which had become a key part of the national culture and identity since it began in 1960. These were the days when soap operas were the kings of the TV schedules, regularly pulling in 15 million viewers for every episode and turning the actors who starred in them into household names.

Everyone I knew watched *Corrie*. If you lived in the North, it was practically the law.

To give you an idea of how influential the show was at its peak, in April 1983 during Manchester United's

League Cup game against Arsenal at Old Trafford, the electronic scoreboard flashed up 'Ken 1 – Mike 0' to inform fans who were missing that night's episode that Deirdre Barlow had chosen to go back to her husband Ken in the love triangle which had gripped the nation.

And in 1998, when Deirdre was wrongfully convicted of fraud and sent to prison, the then Prime Minister Tony Blair intervened in the 'Free the Weatherfield One' campaign, announcing tongue-in-cheek that he would be asking the Home Secretary to look into the matter.

It's totally mad to think of that now because the way we watch TV has completely changed and every soap has seen its audience dwindle, but back in their heyday, millions upon millions were fully invested in the bed-hopping, serial killing and marital drama that were part and parcel of life on the cobbles.

Because *Corrie* was on at 7.30pm, which was my bedtime, I was never allowed to watch it and the famous brass band theme tune striking up was always my signal to go upstairs while Mum and Dad settled down on the sofa with a cup of tea and a custard cream. And woe betide anyone who interrupted once the episode had started. My grandad was particularly strict on that, insisting on total silence as soon as the music started.

So, as *Corrie* devotees, it's fair to say that my whole family was chuffed to pieces that I was now going to be part of it, and my nana and her sister Ivy were especially taken.

'Ooh, our Helen's going to be on *Coronation Street*! What a thing!'

It was even announced by the priest in church and everyone in the congregation broke into a round of applause which I found a bit amusing, but thoroughly enjoyed all the same.

I'd been asked to audition after producers had approached my drama teacher Carol about whether she had any young actresses on her books who might fit the bill to play Sally and Kevin Webster's eldest daughter. Carol had put me forward and my mum drove me to Manchester telling me to give it my best shot, that's all I could do.

I can't actually remember much about the audition in December 1999, just the feeling of knowing that I really, *really* wanted this part – it was way stronger than anything I'd experienced for all previous castings and I don't know why that was. It was like an instinctive sense that this was right for me and something I needed to do.

We drove away from the audition and headed straight to watch my theatre group's pantomime where Carol came running up to us, all giddy.

'You got the part!' she said. 'Well done, Helen, you are the new Rosie Webster!'

The producers had called her in the half an hour since I'd left the audition room so they'd made their minds up sharpish.

The character Rosie was nine, the same age as me in real life and although Sally and Kevin were divorced by the time I started (his explosive affair with Natalie Horrocks played by Denise Welch had ended the marriage a couple of years before), the Websters were still a central and much-loved family on *the Street* which meant I was joining an established set-up.

I would be taking over from the existing actress Emma Collinge who had played Rosie since birth and was leaving to focus on her gymnastics – it's quite common for soap producers to replace younger cast members as they get older and viewers are generally quite forgiving when a character comes down the stairs one day with an entirely new head.

My first day on set came only a few days after my audition, so it was all a bit of a whirlwind with no time for the news to really sink in, but I was desperate to get started. My mum had bought me a new top to wear from (where else?) Tammy Girl which had 'Groovy Chick' emblazoned across the front and I was buzzing with it.

Back then, the show was filmed at the old Granada Studios on Manchester's Quay Street and as I walked through the doors on my first day, I was greeted by a lovely lady with the biggest smile ever who wrapped me up in the warmest of hugs. I remember thinking she was like sunshine.

That lady was Sally Dynevor who played my on-screen mum Sally Webster and I can still feel her beautiful energy now. Sally was never anything but the kindest, loveliest person to work with and after meeting her, any last-minute nerves melted away. I was so eager to get going and there was such a blissful innocence about all that which makes me go all gooey to think of now.

My first scene was with the little girl who played my sister Sophie (Brooke Vincent wouldn't replace her for another two years) as the two of us were trying on our burgundy bridesmaids' dresses for Kevin's wedding to his new partner Alison.

'I'm really excited, I can't wait!'

That was my first line, echoing what I was feeling in real life. And then a very cross Sally came storming into the living room to tell Rosie and Sophie off for not checking with her that it was OK to try on the dresses, before sending us both upstairs to wash our hands.

Rosie and Sophie must have had the cleanest hands in Weatherfield because we were always being sent upstairs to wash them – it became a running joke among the viewers and was even something I got picked on at school for.

'Are you going to wash your hands, *Roooosie*?' If I had a pound for every time I heard that one…

Because I was one of the 'littluns', I had to stay in the kids' room between scenes and I always longed to have access to the green room where all the adults went to chill. The older I got, the more I hated being babied – I was dying to hang out with people like Tina O'Brien, Samia Ghadie and Nikki Sanderson who I thought were the coolest girls ever.

This was when lads' mags like *FHM* and *Nuts* were still flying off the shelves and the soap girls would get to do all these sexy photo shoots which I was in absolute awe of. I wanted to be exactly like them, to be their friend and part of their gang but, of course, I was 10 years younger and just an annoying little kid to them.

I was most starstruck of all by Tracy Shaw who played Maxine Peacock. With her curly blonde hair, sparkly blue eyes and stunning figure, she was so pretty and glamorous and, as a darling of the tabloids at the time, a huge star on and off screen. Her character would eventually become a victim of the serial killer Richard Hillman but she was always so smiley and I idolised her. Kym Marsh (Michelle Connor) was another one who was always kind to me when I was younger and of all the cast, she was probably the one that I would say took me under their wing and looked out for me the most.

I might not have been able to befriend Tina and Nikki, but I did become good mates with Jack P. Shepherd who was only a couple of years older, and started as David Platt a few months after me.

Confession: Jack was my first real crush! I used to think he was really funny – I still do, actually – and so handsome and he was obviously a brilliant little actor to boot. I loved spending time with him and would even look forward to the four hours of tutoring we were legally required to do on the days we were working because it meant I got to breathe the same air as him.

When on set, I had a lovely chaperone called Jenny who was always super kind to me although she did shout at me once for repeating a joke I hadn't realised was inappropriate and I don't think I've ever fully recovered. She used to wear pearl earrings, pink lipstick and lots of mascara so her eyelashes were phenomenal. I loved my tutor Kit, as well, although I think I was the only *Corrie* kid who actually did their schoolwork.

Right from the off, it felt like a family, a home from home and even though I was doing scenes with proper legends like John Savident (Fred Elliott) and Barbara Knox (Rita Fairclough), it became the norm for me. I was so young, so I don't think I really grasped the magnitude of it all, which was probably a good thing.

The character Rita was very close to the Websters and a bit like Rosie and Sophie's surrogate nan, so I had a lot of scenes with her. Barbara Knox is a fabulous, formidable woman, a national treasure and still full of sass and glamour now in her 90s, but she could also be quite scary if she thought you weren't behaving in a professional manner. I remember her shouting at me when I checked with the director what I was meant to say next.

'Don't you learn your lines?' she boomed.

I was 27 by then but I still just about shit myself.

Being on set was a novelty which never wore off. When Brooke joined the cast in 2002, we would often deliberately fluff our lines because we wanted to stay on a little bit longer. I was a little bit jealous of Brooke at first because, as the new girl, she got a lot of fuss made of her. She was also a really good actress and suddenly I had a bit of competition and had to up my game. She could cry on cue, a skill I'd never been able to master, and I found that really irritating.

But it didn't take long for me to get over my initial doubts about her and me and Brooke soon became really close. She's still one of my best mates and she's been there for me when I've needed her over the years.

Those days at *Corrie* were my favourite days. Without wanting to sound over-the-top, it felt like this was my calling. This was my thing and I wanted to do it forever.

* * *

I was halfway through Year Five when I started on *Corrie* and school was still a daily chore for me, something I had to endure rather than enjoy.

To get through in order to get out.

Apart from the Great Silver Rain Controversy which had massively dented my confidence and left me isolated, I was struggling with the work and especially maths which I wasn't able to get a handle on at all. It felt as if everyone else was racing ahead, sailing through every lesson while I was lagging behind, flailing, confused and unable to understand even the basics.

In Year Six a teacher suggested I get my sight tested and it was discovered that I needed glasses, so a major part of my learning problems had been because I couldn't see what was being written on the board. My prescription today is minus six so I'm just about as blind as a bat.

Bullying, loneliness and difficulties in lessons – it all made for a great deal of misery. By the time I left primary school in July 2001, my overwhelming feeling was one of relief because the last two years had been so unhappy.

I was hopeful of finding a fresh start at Thornleigh Salesian College, a Roman Catholic secondary school in Bolton's Astley Edge. And the early signs were positive – I got quite a lot of attention for being on *Coronation Street* and settled in quickly to the social side of school, making a decent bunch of friends. But even though I was fairly happy during that first year at Thornleigh, I was still very young for my age and, compared to a lot of the other more streetwise kids, hopelessly naïve thanks to the pretty sheltered upbringing I'd had. I was almost 12 years old and still believed in Santa Claus. Not even joking.

I also struggled to apply myself to schoolwork and by the end of Year Seven, found myself placed in all the bottom sets, which was really upsetting – I'd always been a geek at heart, a 'good girl', and had no desire to be stuck down there. It ended up being a bit of a wake-up call and I knew I was going to have to seriously up my efforts in Year Eight or risk being consigned to the lower ability groups.

Resolving to smash it, I worked my arse off and clawed my way back into the top sets, which on one hand I was pleased about, but on the other, it meant I was now labelled a swot. The early buzz of popularity from *Corrie* had started to wear off and instead I became a target again.

For the next year I was bullied *relentlessly*. Sometimes it would be physical and I'd get roughed up, but mostly it was verbal and it made me retreat back into my protective shell again. There was one girl who I was scared of more than anyone and she'd deliberately humiliate me by asking me sexual questions in front of all the boys. I was a late developer and puberty hadn't really hit me at that point (I had no boobs until 17 and didn't start my periods until 15) and she asked me if I had any 'pubes'.

I didn't have a clue what she meant or how to respond, but the whole class was howling laughing at me and although it's funny when I talk about it now, at the time it was horrible. This is more than 20 years ago, but those feelings of shame have stayed with me and are as real now as they were then. I came home that evening and asked my mum what pubes were and she wouldn't tell me!

I'd get called frigid and 'boff head' and teased for my 'skater girl' style which was thanks to my love affair with Avril Lavigne. I attempted some self-preservation tactics and even once tried to befriend the girl who was making my life hell, thinking if I could get her onside then the bullying would stop. It's so cringe to think of now, but I told her she looked like Catherine Zeta-Jones, trying to flatter her, desperate to find peace.

Needless to say, it didn't bloody work!

I just wasn't built for the rough and tumble of secondary school. Although the fact I was on telly was often used as something to pick on me for, I think I would have been bullied regardless of *Corrie*. I was a softie. Small for my age, very innocent, a little bit quirky and an easy target in a school where it was all about survival of the fittest.

I was also probably a bit more well-spoken than some of the other kids because I'd had elocution lessons for drama and so that got me labelled 'posh' and a 'rich bitch' even though I couldn't have been further away from that.

I buried myself in my schoolwork and went back to how I'd been in the last two years of primary school; a loner, an introvert and trying to keep my head down. I'd come home every evening and watch *Harry Potter and the Chamber of Secrets* like a total saddo – that movie became like a security blanket for me.

The school was rubbish at supporting or protecting me and there was one class which is seared into my memory where I was bullied non-stop for an hour while the teacher just looked on and did nothing.

My parents noticed the stark difference in me between Years Seven and Eight and expressed some concern.

'Helen, what's wrong with you?' Mum asked once. 'You don't speak anymore.'

I couldn't find the words to tell her what was going on. At the time, my brother Tom was beginning to grapple with various troubles. To me, he was my cool big brother and a lot of fun to be around, but he had his demons and Mum and Dad were constantly worried about him. On some level, I was conscious of not wanting to be an extra burden when they already had enough to deal with, but my anxiety was cranking up. Eventually, towards the end of Year Eight, I broke down and cried to my parents, begging them to let me move schools. I told them I was 'stressed' which made my dad laugh.

'You don't know what stress is,' he said.

But they definitely realised how dispirited school was making me and, thankfully, agreed things couldn't go on the way they were. I'd had my heart set on moving to Westholme School in Blackburn, but it was fee-paying and there was no way my mum and dad could afford the several thousands of pounds it cost a term.

So it was decided that we would use my wages from *Corrie* to fund the fees and as long as I got through the entrance exams, I could move there for the start of Year Nine.

I had to pass English, maths, French and science to get in and knowing this was my chance to escape Thornleigh, I knuckled right down, with Mum and Dad kindly paying for some extra tutoring to help me over the line.

The day I found out my application had been successful was one of sheer joy and when I started at Westholme in September 2003, I absolutely loved it from day one. It was all girls which I was probably better suited to and I just fitted in straight away.

I'd come from a school where you were bullied for working hard and being a geek, but this place was the complete opposite because the cleverest and most studious pupils were the most popular.

The whole ethos at Westholme, which was set in gorgeous countryside with a woodland walk and a little river running through the grounds, was geared around driving students to be successful, independent young women. They pushed you to be ambitious for yourself and your future career and I responded so well to that, rediscovering the confidence and self-belief that had been pummelled out of me in the previous schools.

I was surrounded by a lot of extremely academic kids and although I wasn't naturally clever and it was often hard to keep up with my classmates and the expectations of the school, I had a strong work ethic and a determination to do well. My friends, who had all benefited from the advantages of a private education from a much younger age, sailed through most subjects with straight As, while I would be lucky to scrape a B. Or a C when it came to maths and science.

I didn't like sports and there was a lot of emphasis placed on sporting prowess – I think we had an Olympic swimmer in the school and someone who had swum the bloody Channel. How do you live up to those standards?

But I was enjoying school life again and although there wasn't a subject I excelled in, I was quite good at English, so I got by. My GCSEs in 2006 were a mix of Bs, As and A*s so in the grand scheme of things, I did really well.

I was different to a lot of the Westholme girls, though. Many of them came from wealthy families and were used to privileged lifestyles where money was no object. The dad of one of the girls in my class had his own helicopter which was, like, WOAH. I thought that was so cool.

The fact I was on *Corrie* was neither here nor there to anyone, the other girls could not have cared less – I think when your parents are absolutely loaded, that sort of thing doesn't impress or even remotely bother you.

I became very good friends with a beautiful girl called Maddie who is still one of my ride or dies today. She lived in a massive house in Chorley and her mum had the most amazing designer handbag collection known to man. I'd never seen anything like it in the flesh before and I was fascinated by the Louis Vuittons and Chloes on display.

I told myself that when I was older, I was going to have my own collection and that's something I did indeed start from the age of about 16, with a white Chloe Paddington I still have now and then saving up every month until I had enough to buy the next target on my most wanted list.

* * *

The start of my days at Westholme coincided with an upping of the ante over at *Corrie* and some significant character development for Rosie. I'd spent the first couple of years bedding in, getting used to the surroundings and becoming a familiar face to the viewers. The producers had always been careful not to overload me with anything too taxing.

Now, in a strange case of art imitating life, my first big storyline involved Rosie switching from her comp Weatherfield High to Oakhill, a private school, a move orchestrated by Sally, who had lofty ambitions for her daughter and felt that state education was holding her back. Rosie was adamant that she didn't want to move and it spelled for some huge rows between her and Sally which I loved getting my teeth into!

There were some scenes I wasn't keen on at all, though. Sally had become this pushy stagey mother who wanted Rosie to become a star and at one audition I had to get up and sing 'Somewhere Over The Rainbow' on the stage with my hair in pigtails and I *hated* it. I was so embarrassed, but sometimes it's necessary to suffer for art, darling!

I was becoming a more prominent member of the cast, being trusted with meatier storylines and it was when Rosie decided to become a goth that the character really took off. If you watched it, you might remember how horrendous I looked in this scraggy old black wig which was hideous. I was absolutely fuming when it was handed to me! I'm naturally fair and together with my blonde eyebrows, which I'd plucked into oblivion (this was the noughties, after all), the whole look was completely ridiculous.

I despised that horrible wig so much I ended up dying my own hair black so I no longer had to wear it.

The make-up artists who were like my aunties were forever telling me off because I had to be pale to be a Goth, but I didn't want to look all pasty. By now I was properly into my fake tan and I'd turn up to work looking like I'd just had a fortnight on a Mediterranean beach…

'Helen, you're supposed to be as white as a sheet, for goodness sake!' they'd say in despair and then try to douse me in white powder to gothify me.

This was all tied up with Rosie getting her first boyfriend, Craig Harris, who lived at number six and was played by Richard Fleeshman. Love's young dream, they were.

Oh my god, Richard Fleeshman.

Richard. Fucking. Fleeshman.

I was madly in love with him. Like, obsessed. Our first kissing scene in 2005, when I was 14, had the two of us perched on the side of the street and I was so excited beforehand because I thought he was the fittest lad ever. I'd only kissed one other boy before that, a year earlier at an under-16s night at Atlantis nightclub in Bolton where me and my friends would all go out in our tiny Miss Sixty skirts thinking we were 'it'. Someone told me afterwards he'd only snogged me because I was in *Coronation Street* and that comment stayed with me.

Anyway, I was now required to kiss Richard Fleeshman

on a regular basis and I was delighted with life. All the girls in my school fancied him, he was such a big heart-throb at the time and they were so jealous that not only did I get to kiss him, but I was being paid to do it.

On school time!

I mean, getting a day off maths to go and snog the face off Richard Fleeshman? I didn't think life could get any sweeter.

I must add that although I was head over heels for Richard, it was totally unrequited. He couldn't have been less interested in me – he was only a year older, but to him I was just this silly little girl he happened to work with and who still needed a chaperone on set.

We once had a conversation about whether I had a boyfriend and I said to him, 'Oh, I just want someone like you...' only to be met with an awkward silence. Ouch.

Bless little Helen! Richard didn't want to hang out with me; he only wanted to be with the older, cooler girls and boys in the cast. There was an actress called Zaraah Abrahams who played Joanna Jackson and one day after filming she went off shopping with Richard in town and I was *devo*. That's what a crush is like, isn't it? You obsess over and analyse every conversation and it's agony when you realise they barely notice you.

Nevertheless, every time Rosie and Craig had a romantic scene, I'd spend the whole evening before exfoliating, shaving and moisturising while Jane, my older sister, mercilessly took the piss out of me.

When Rosie and Craig decided to sleep with each other for the first time, I was still a virgin in real life, but couldn't think of a better way to spend my time – ha!

As the plot around their relationship ramped up, I was summoned to a meeting with the *Coronation Street* producer Tony Wood, one I knew Richard had also been told to attend. I was so excited and persuaded my mum to let me go to River Island where I treated myself to a new outfit just for this meeting – a black waistcoat and matching trousers which I thought were so chic.

The meeting was scheduled for straight after my tutoring session, but I nipped back to my dressing room first to cover my face in Hula Benefit bronzer – Richard was going to be there, after all! – which meant that I was about 10 minutes late.

Not a good start.

Tony Wood was absolutely seething and properly screamed at me about how unprofessional and rude it was to keep him waiting and how dare I behave in such an entitled manner. If I hadn't been so blindsided by this, I would have burst into tears on the spot, but I was too shocked to react and I genuinely can't remember a single word of the meeting that followed.

When we left the room, Richard was horrified for me.

'Helen, are you OK?' he asked.

I definitely wasn't. That's when the tears sprung and I couldn't stop crying for the rest of the day, every time it popped into my head, I'd be overcome. I know I was in the wrong for being a few minutes late and Tony was fully justified in being a bit ticked off, but I don't think it's appropriate for a powerful middle-aged man – the big boss of the whole show – to do that to a 14-year-old girl who was only guilty of making a daft mistake.

If he'd just said, 'Helen, timekeeping is really important and being late isn't acceptable. Please make sure it doesn't happen again,' that would have sent the message loud and clear without causing any distress.

I told my parents when I got home that night and my dad was so mad he wanted to come down to the studio the next day and speak to Tony himself.

'I'm not having it!' he said. 'He doesn't speak to my daughter like that and reduce her to tears.'

However, my mum talked him out of it, worried that I'd lose my job because Tony could always have me written out of the show. After that meeting I felt extremely uncomfortable around him – not frightened as such, but definitely on edge. It makes me quite angry to think of now and if it happened today I'd call him a knobhead and walk out.

* * *

Unfortunately for me, a major stumbling block to my plan to run off into the sunset with Richard Fleeshman was his girlfriend. He'd got together with Roxanne Pallett who he'd met while starring on *Soapstar Superstar*, an *X Factor*-style ITV talent show which featured various soapstars singing for public votes. Roxanne played Jo Stiles in *Emmerdale* and she and Richard became quite the celebrity couple even though at 23, she was seven years older than him which I always thought was a bit odd.

The two of them had been dating for a few months when one evening, I was at home and the house phone rang.

'Helen,' my dad shouted up to my room, 'Roxanne's on the phone for you.'

This came as a surprise; me and her weren't mates and only knew each other in passing, so I was a bit confused as I picked up the receiver. I instantly realised that this wasn't a call for a friendly chat – she was furious.

'Stop telling everyone you're in love with my boyfriend!' she shouted down the line. 'He doesn't even like you!'

And then she slammed the phone down leaving me shaking. How random is that? She was a grown-ass woman of 23, why would she feel so insecure that she needed to ring up a 15-year-old schoolgirl to issue a warning like that? I still can't get my head round it.

Years later in 2018, long after she'd split from Richard, Roxanne got into a load of trouble with her appearance on *Celebrity Big Brother* when she accused Ryan Thomas (who played Jason Grimshaw in *Corrie*) of physically assaulting her in the *CBB* house. The incident became known as 'Punchgate' when the cameras proved that she wasn't telling the truth and had overreacted to what was clearly a couple of seconds of gentle play-fighting with no malice whatsoever attached.

Punchgate was all over the papers and social media for days and it saw Roxanne torn to shreds – what happened to her in the aftermath didn't rest well with me at all. It doesn't take away from the fact that what she did to Ryan was totally wrong and could have ended his career, but the way it was handled by *Big Brother* and the press was terrible. She was branded the 'most hated woman in Britain' and it was horrible to watch her eviction interview with host Emma Willis in front of a TV audience baying for blood, almost like we'd regressed to the days of public hangings. The overall tone and line of questioning towards a woman who was clearly in a very fragile place felt, to me at least, unnecessarily aggressive.

I was never Roxanne's biggest fan, but no one deserves that. I know what it's like when the media comes for you when you're at the centre of a storm, and it's frightening. Unfortunately, it's often part and parcel of being in the public eye.

Fame wasn't something I really *noticed* happening because it happened so gradually. When I started on *Corrie*, I was either in school, on set or at my drama class – that was literally my life and I didn't really go anywhere else. As I got older, I'd go into town with my friends and every so often someone would come up and ask for an autograph – this was before the days when every phone came with a camera and so there was no such thing as a selfie. Happier times!

But there were often photographers hanging about outside the studios and once I hit 16 I'd be snapped arriving at and leaving work, and was regularly featured in the papers which was always good fun. The press were generally quite kind to me back then and it was part of the job I enjoyed.

As I was becoming one of the more grown-up members of the cast, I no longer needed a chaperone and could, at long last, join everyone else in the green room – the births of my children aside, the first time I crossed the hallowed threshold remains one of the greatest days of my life.

They could honestly do a reality TV show about what goes on in the *Coronation Street* green room: who's sleeping with who, who's fallen out with who, who's pissed off with the producers and threatening to quit… to say it lived up to my expectations and then some would be an understatement! I bloody loved it in there.

I was right into the glamorous side of the job. I didn't come from a showbiz family or have any previous experience of this lifestyle, so I found it all quite other worldly and I became very conscious of my image and how I looked. This probably stemmed from being in an all-girls' school but it was definitely exacerbated by the pressures of being in the spotlight and being around all the pretty stars on *Corrie* which could feel like being in a permanent beauty pageant. Social media wasn't the beast it is today, but there was always the possibility of being papped in Manchester and there were regular red-carpet events to attend where you'd be snapped from all angles and to within an inch of your life.

Those pressures were never more acute than at the annual Soap Awards, the biggest, glitziest date in the television calendar… and also the most badly behaved night of the year. I can't tell you how much time, prep and discussion went into the build-up – amongst the younger cast members at least, it was the only topic of conversation for weeks beforehand.

In 2006 it was my first year attending as a senior member of the cast and I'd been nominated for Best Dramatic Performance so knew there would be a lot of eyes on me that night.

I had a gorgeous pink dress which I'd bought from Harvey Nichols and I was really looking forward to the do, but wracked with nerves and insecurities at the same time. The truth is, I'd starved myself to fit into that dress. My food habits were growing increasingly erratic as I caved to the strains of life in the limelight.

And within weeks of walking down that red carpet at the Soap Awards, I would be in the grip of a full-blown eating disorder.

Chapter Three

Off the Rails

I DIDN'T JUST WANT TO lose the teenage puppy fat, the aim was to be skinny. Really, *really* skinny. That was basically my main goal in life, to be as teeny tiny as possible.

The willowy Sienna Miller was my idol and I thought if only I could be thin like her, I'd look beautiful and feel more confident and maybe the boys would notice me. I can see how crazy and damaging that is now, but it was all-consuming at the time and at school I was around a fair amount of competitive dieting – the peer pressure and comparison culture combined was a toxic force.

I'd grown up watching my mum constantly calorie-counting, she was always on WeightWatchers, keeping tabs on her points or trying some faddy diet or other and I'd sub-consciously internalised all of that. The desire to be slim was pretty normal to me.

HEAD & HEART

In the run-up to the Soap Awards in May 2006 and fitting into the pink Harvey Nicks dress, I'd started experimenting with bingeing and starving myself and unsurprisingly, my eating patterns became seriously fucked up. I might have a bowl of ice cream for breakfast which, in my warped logic, meant I'd used up my entire, self-imposed daily 'allowance' in one go and therefore couldn't eat anything else for the rest of the day.

That's when I'd starve.

I tried making myself sick, but could never manage to bring anything up, so starvation was my go-to plan. I'd survive on coffee and maybe an apple, but only if I got desperately hungry.

Between the Soap Awards in May and the Inside Soap Awards four months later, I dropped from a size eight to a four and lost so much weight I was now under seven stone.

I was painfully, horribly thin and when I look at pictures of that time, it's crystal clear how ill I was. I was skeletal, nothing more than skin and bone – I wore a backless blue dress to the Inside Soap Awards and thought it looked great, but you can see my spine jutting out, for God's sake. My arms were so emaciated, it looked as if you could get your finger and thumb around them.

And yet, I was euphoric that my efforts were paying off and vowed to keep my weight below seven stone forever. I weighed myself every day and swam 100 lengths in the gym pool each morning, surviving mostly on fruit cordial and cups of powdered soup.

I'd also started to scratch myself.

I want to be really careful with how I describe exactly what was going on here and I'd hesitate to give it a label. I wasn't actually cutting into my flesh – I never drew blood – and this was a very short phase in a particularly chaotic time of my life.

But I do recognise now that it was a form of self-harm. It was a cry for help and an attempt, I guess, to relieve some of the tension I was living with. I think a lot of this was probably linked to my hormones and what I now know to be PMDD – Premenstrual Dysphoric Disorder. I'd just started my periods and they've given me two decades of grief ever since which I'm going to talk more about later on.

I'd sit in my room and scratch my arms and wrists with a pair of scissors or a knife. The make-up ladies at *Corrie* noticed the marks and I had to make up some excuse about being got at by a friend's overly-playful cat... I'm not sure if they bought it, but nothing was ever followed up and no one asked me about it again.

I knew my parents were worried about me. They didn't know the extent of the mental anguish I was experiencing or how deep my issues went, but they could see I was wasting away and my mum would plead with me to eat something. They contacted the school and the nurse got involved, putting me and a few other girls who also had an eating disorder, under her care. I'd have a regular appointment with her where we'd discuss what was going on, but there was no talking to me at that time; my anorexia was dictating the play.

There was also a meeting called with *Corrie* because the bosses had grown frustrated with what they saw as my struggle to concentrate on set although no one had joined the dots and connected this to my drastic weight loss.

'That's because she doesn't eat!' my mum said to the producers and I was mad with her for ratting me out like that.

After that, and at her wits' end, she took me to The Priory clinic in Altrincham as an outpatient and I started having weekly therapy sessions with a counsellor.

As we worked through a lot of the noise in my head and started to unpick some of my thought processes, my poor concentration and habitual clumsiness kept on cropping up. My focus had always been bad and especially so if it was a lesson I wasn't really interested in. I was OK with the creative subjects like English, drama and, weirdly, RE, but useless at anything logical or scientific. On the flip side, when I loved something, I'd hyper focus on it to the point of obsession – prime example, Richard Fleeshman.

I was also incredibly forgetful and I'd lose things all the time which drove the *Corrie* prop team wild.

As a result of the digging we did in my counselling sessions, shortly before my 17th birthday, I was diagnosed with Attention Deficit Hyperactivity Disorder (ADHD) which meant very little to me at the time but the more I found out about it, the more it made sense to me. All my life I'd been 'away with the fairies' but now I had a reason for my scatterbrain and distractedness and it wasn't because there was anything 'wrong' with me.

Being prescribed methylphenidate (more commonly known under the brand names Ritalin or Concerta, which is the one I was given), changed everything almost immediately. I'm sure it took a while to truly kick in, but to me it felt instantly revolutionary, like having this clarity for the first time.

You might have seen the Bradley Cooper film *Limitless* where his character plays a struggling author who is given this new drug which promises to help him with his creative problems. Under the influence of this pill, he's transformed into a genius with the ability to speak multiple languages fluently, successfully play the stock market and write a novel in a few days.

Now, I'm not saying my ADHD meds turned me into a rocket scientist, but they did give me the ability to think straight without any fuzziness, something I'd been finding problematic for years. To me it was a wonder drug, my saviour and the solution to all my problems.

What I didn't realise then was that this little pill, which appeared to be my all-singing, all-dancing cure, would also be my undoing. Over the next few years I would develop a dependency on it which would take me to the edge of sanity and then come to a head in the most devastating of ways.

* * *

I know I'm an actress and I had a job to do at *Corrie*, but when your self-worth is so connected to your body image, it's hard to separate the fiction from the personal.

There were some very difficult days at work and a scene where Michelle Keegan, who played Tina McIntyre, had to call Rosie 'chubby' in a fight sent me into a tailspin.

Michelle had joined the cast in January 2008, and although she was only a year older than me, she was noticeably much more together and worldly-wise. Naturally beautiful, confident and comfortable in her own skin, she was loved instantly by everyone on and off screen.

I used to find it so embarrassing when we were pitted against each other for the Sexiest Female awards because obviously she was going to win and I'd end up feeling humiliated and dreadful about myself. I wanted nothing more than for them to stop putting me up for those categories especially when my self-esteem was already a tricky thing. The Soap Awards did away with those 'Sexiest' awards after 2014, perhaps recognising how harmful and sexist they could be.

I must add that I liked Michelle as a person and got on well with her. There was no competition or animosity between us, but I was constantly paranoid about my weight, my looks… everything.

I didn't help matters. I was often my own worst enemy and a law unto myself. There were some proper rows with my mum and she'd despair of me as I started to go off the rails. I'd been such a good little Catholic girl up until I was about 16, but being in the public eye opened up opportunities and I began going out in Manchester where the nightlife offered bright lights and excitement. We'd go to the Sugar Lounge in Deansgate where all the soapstars and celebs would be given the VIP treatment which I found intoxicating. I was 'Rosie Webster off *Corrie*' which meant I was a name and a face in there and had status, dressed in something minuscule from Miss Sixty with my latest designer handbag on my arm.

I'm squirming at myself just remembering!

My parents didn't have time to keep a close eye on what I was getting up to because they were preoccupied with my brother and I took full advantage of that – I was able to come and go from the house more or less as I pleased, and at whatever time I fancied without much questioning.

There were occasions, however, when my mum bu and that would descend into an argument. Our relationship, which had once been so close, was coming apart at the seams and there were times when I really felt like I hated her. We would have proper screaming matches over the smallest things.

HEAD & HEART

My mum was trying to do the right thing, but I didn't want to be under any sort of control and that's how I saw her, as this unreasonable, obstructive force who didn't understand me.

Things eventually deteriorated to the point that we were barely speaking. I was permanently angry with her and thought all my problems were her fault, while she'd tell me I was making her ill with worry.

I hated that she made me feel like I was different, or that I was to blame for her struggling. Who did she think she was, telling me I wasn't well and that there was something wrong with me?

I can see now that she'd already been to hell and back with my brother and was terrified I was heading the same way, although I have *never* and would never take illegal drugs. I've been around them enough to see how they destroy lives and it's not a path I will ever go down myself.

She was right to be worried about what I was getting up to, though. Every time I went out to party, I'd drink heavily, getting wasted on Jagerbombs and whatever else I could lay my hands on, often landing myself in some horrible, potentially dangerous situations.

Like the night I was out in Bolton with friends from school and got chatting in a bar to a bloke who was old enough to be my dad. It was early on in the night, but I was already paralytic drunk when he offered to drive us to the restaurant we were going to for a meal and when we arrived, he joined us at the table. He sat next to me and started touching my leg and then feeling me up before asking me to go home with him.

How gross is that? I was only bloody 16! Luckily there were plenty of other people around and I shouted at him to get his hands off me which scared him away and he scarpered.

Although I'd never gone further than a drunken snog with anyone, I was getting a lot of male attention when I went out and my first real date was with a young footballer who was playing for Manchester United at the time. It was the autumn of 2006 and I'd just started sixth form – he was 19, three years older than me, and I thought he was the most beautiful guy I'd ever seen.

I used to think being a footballer's wife was really glamorous – Coleen Rooney was a big name and I thought she must have such a lovely life. In fact, Michael le Vell who played my on-screen dad, used to ask me what I wanted to be when I grew up and I'd always reply, 'a WAG!'

And so when I heard that this guy wanted to take me out, I thought all my birthdays and Christmases had come at once.

Oh my God, I'm going on a date with a Man United player! And he's so handsome!

It was a Monday night and he came to pick me up from my parents' house, pulling up in this fancy white sports car and we drove into Manchester where he paid for an expensive dinner at a restaurant just opposite the *Corrie* studios. I thought he was *amazing*.

We shared a kiss at the end of the night when he dropped me home and I was on cloud nine. Floating! We had a couple more dates over the next few weeks but I held off sleeping with him, not daft enough to think I was the only girl he was taking out – as footballers go, he was one of the worst when it came to that.

God, I was desperate to lose my virginity, though. I'd become really good friends with Emma Rigby who played Hannah Ashworth in *Hollyoaks* and I kind of fell in love with her. It was an intense friendship and we were besotted with each other. I just wanted to be like her – everything Emma did I would then want to do. I started getting my nails French manicured like hers and my eyebrows professionally done.

She also had a Hollywood wax which I started getting done at Harvey Nicks as well.

I think I became infatuated with Emma who was such a beautiful girl (she still is) and so when she told me she'd lost her virginity, I became even more determined to get rid of mine, too. I wanted to be a grown-up and to be able to tell my friends I'd had sex, which makes me feel quite sad to remember that now.

It eventually happened the night I'd been to a *Hollyoaks* party at some venue in Manchester and got talking to a guy who was a 6ft 4in model and totally stunning. He was 20, four years older than me and after the party, he took me to a hotel in Bolton where I had sex for the first time. It wasn't the greatest experience for me, it was painful and afterwards he told me that he wouldn't tell anyone because he didn't want me to 'get a name' for myself.

That made me feel cheap. What a thoughtless thing to say to a girl, especially after taking her virginity. I wish to God that I'd lost it in a 'nicer' way, but the fact is I was reckless with it and ended up sleeping with a guy who was a bit of a knob.

I know loads of women regret their first time and you might well be reading this and relating to what I'm describing, but it's made me want so much more for my daughters which is why I'm an open book with them. I hope they feel they can talk to me about anything.

My mum would never have dreamed of discussing sex with me, I think she would have keeled over with embarrassment! She wanted to keep me as a baby and she simply couldn't deal with any conversation which strayed into intimacy or bodily functions.

I mean, she wouldn't even tell me what a pube was!

As a result, I developed quite a strong sense of shame around sex and it's another reason why I'm determined to do things differently with my own children. As my daughters Matilda and Delilah get older, I want them to know that sex is a precious thing and it's worth waiting for the right person. Save it for someone who's kind and genuinely cares about you, not just any old random because your virginity feels like a burden rather than something to be treasured.

I didn't learn my lesson after that underwhelming and uncomfortable first time because a few weeks later, I bumped into the Man United footballer again in the Sugar Lounge and went back to his place at the end of the night. I was really drunk and wearing a barely-there dress, the kind which would send my mum into a frenzy whenever she saw me papped in the papers.

'For god's sake, Helen!' she'd say. 'Look at Tina O'Brien, she always looks so classy. And there's you with your boobs out again!'

I had sex with the footballer that night and remember telling him that I wanted him to look after me. To him, 'looking after me' meant phoning for a taxi to take me home – he basically got what he wanted from me and then sent me packing which was a horrible feeling and one I didn't want to repeat. I promised myself never to have another one-night stand again and that was something I would stick to for nearly 20 years.

* * *

Towards the end of 2006, Richard Fleeshman had announced he was quitting *Coronation Street* to pursue a career in music which obviously spelled the end for Rosie and Craig. Violins!

Although I was sad that he was leaving the cast, it was probably the best thing that could have happened for me personally because I still had this massive, pointless crush on the boy and it had all become so difficult for me. Quite upsetting, really. I was only 16 and thought I was in love with him which meant I often found our relationship confusing as I wrestled with those feelings.

Richard's exit storyline centred around Craig and Rosie's plan to run away to Berlin together following a romantic trip to Paris. At the last minute, just as they were about to board the train to Germany, Rosie had second thoughts and backed out, not wanting to leave her family behind in Weatherfield and we had to film these highly emotional farewell scenes in the middle of the Gare du Nord.

That sounds so exhilarating when I think about it now – shooting the end of an epic love story in the heart of Paris was a dream! But, for me at least, it was genuinely tough to do and my tears as we said our goodbyes were real.

And that was it. He was off. He didn't look back.

For a while I felt a little lost without Richard to lust over although it was also quite liberating. Craig's departure paved the way for Rosie's evolution and without a steady boyfriend, she was free to come into her own, to transform into a fully-fledged character and be given much more significant and weighty storylines.

But while I knew the producers had big plans for her, I could never have predicted the John Stape affair and kidnapping which would become one of the *Street's* most memorable and controversial plots and one that is still talked about today.

I can't remember being given any advance warning about what was going to happen. I literally opened the script one day and thought, 'What the actual fuck?!'

It all kicked off in the summer of 2007 after Rosie had dropped out of school and was working as a PA at the Underworld knicker factory. John was a much older teacher at Weatherfield High and the boyfriend of Fiz Brown from number five, and he and Rosie met while he was giving English Literature tutoring to Sally, who was studying for an A Level as a mature student.

Over the autumn of 2007, Rosie and John became embroiled in this illicit affair which was amazing being at the centre of such a big storyline, but also felt very strange doing love scenes with a man who was twice my age. I didn't relish that.

The actor who played John, Graham Hawley, was in his mid-thirties and I think it must have been fairly uncomfortable for him too, having to passionately kiss a teenager – and an immature one at that – although I must say he was always very nice with me and a real professional.

The story built to a crescendo on Christmas Day 2007 (I was buzzing to get the Christmas Day episode which always pulled in a huge audience) when the affair was revealed, John was exposed and his life fell apart.

After that, he was fired from his teaching post and

forced to take a job as a cabbie, and blaming Rosie for everything he'd lost, he kidnapped her, locking her in his dead grandmother's house for several weeks. We filmed those scenes in a real basement, and it felt like being on a movie set – I am super grateful to have had those opportunities to hone my skills as an actress at such a young age.

By now Rosie had transformed from silly schoolgirl to full-blown seductress, and I was generally OK with the way things had gone for the character. She was a right little minx and often fun to play, but it also meant there were scenes with a series of older male actors which didn't always sit comfortably with me. Not even years later during my second stint on *Corrie*, when I was in my mid-20s – a grown woman now with a child in real life – I had to film a bedroom scene with an actor in his 60s. Obviously it was pre-watershed so all quite tame, but I felt minging post-shoot.

After John Stape came factory boss Tony Gordon who was in his 40s and played by Gray O'Brien. I was still only 18 and we shot it in a hotel with me dressed in this skimpy corset and knickers, attempting to seduce him and I found it embarrassing, but I played the femme fatale well.

It's not like the actors were ever creepy with me, but I was conflicted. I *wanted* to have the main storylines. I wanted to be one of the big actresses, on a par with Tina and Nikki, so I was never going to refuse or kick up a fuss. It was my job and part of me enjoyed the kudos of being seen as attractive – I was flattered to be regarded as sexy enough to pull it off – and I loved being in the thick of something that was getting people talking.

I was getting the good storylines and, when push came to shove, I thought that was the only thing that mattered.

On the other hand, was it morally right that I was expected to parade about in my knickers like some mad nymphomaniac when I was still just a teenager? Alison King, who plays Carla Connor, once kicked off once in the green room to another actor saying how disgusting it was that they were sexualising me when I was a young girl and I didn't fully comprehend what she was talking about at the time.

I do now. I get it.

The whole John Stape 'affair' portrayed Rosie as the orchestrater when, in fact, he was the older man in a position of power and she was only 17. I'm not sure they'd write it in quite the same way all these years later and since the #MeToo movement. There is much more awareness now about how abusers operate and how damaging it is for survivors to be blamed or disbelieved – Rosie might have been a consenting adult in the eyes of the law, but John was undoubtedly a groomer who deserved no sympathy.

My my eyes are wide open to all this now. There have been so many times in my career that I've just gone along with jobs I wasn't totally happy with because I was a people pleaser and thought it would be unprofessional to object. I remember doing a shoot for a betting brand once, I'd had no briefing for it and when I got to the studio, which was decked out as a horse stable, I realised the styling was me in a skimpy red leotard and armed with a whip.

They wanted me to get into some very suggestive positions; it felt sordid, tacky and I didn't want to be told by a man with a camera to bend over and flash my cleavage while posing with a whip. But I still did it.

These days I do loads of lingerie campaigns and I think it's great to show that mums in their 30s can be confident and sexy. But they are all shoots where I'm in control, it's my decision and I'm fully aware of what I'm doing. I don't mind being sexual as long as I'm the one calling the shots.

Whatever the rights and wrongs of how Rosie's 'man-eating' behaviour was written, the John Stape saga did indeed raise my public profile and there was a big uptick in media interest which I was chuffed about. The team in the *Corrie* press office would always laugh because I was so eager to do the magazine photoshoots on my days off.

By now I had my first serious boyfriend, a good-looking lad called Danny Scott who worked for a builder's merchant and was a few years older than me. He had his head screwed on and my parents were glad that I'd found a bit of calm amongst the chaos – having this steady relationship meant I wasn't going out getting drunk in Manchester with a load of wrong'uns.

Me and Danny had met in the gym when I was really struggling with my eating disorder and he turned out to be a good distraction from what was crashing about in my head. He kind of levelled me out and he was always super sweet – just a nice, normal, grounded guy from Bolton and probably exactly what I needed at that time.

He was good for me. Over the years we were together, the eating disorder which had once been so inescapable started to peter out. I wouldn't say I had a completely healthy relationship with food, but I broke the binging and starving loop and was comfortable when I started to gain some weight.

That was a million miles from where I'd been before I met him.

We had an offer from *OK!* magazine to do a couples shoot together which I practically bit their hand off for. I could have wet myself with excitement because *OK!* shoots were always a lot of fun to do, you got a set of lovely pictures out of them, a nice interview and they paid good money, but I think I would have done it for free, I was that thrilled.

We shot it at Stanley House in the Ribble Valley countryside and it was more like a wedding shoot which was fine by me because at that stage I was madly in love and totally convinced we were going to get married. I wanted us to move in together and managed to find this lovely apartment to rent just down the road from my parents' house.

It felt incredibly grown-up to be living with a boy although I really was still just a kid. I always wanted to be older than I was.

It was around this time that I sacked off my A Levels, walking out of my first exam and never returning, something I've regretted ever since. I'd been studying psychology, English language, English literature and drama at Westholme's sixth form, but my head hadn't been in the game for a long time and I dread to think what my results would have looked like if I'd gone ahead and actually sat the exams.

Me and Danny lived in each other's pockets and he'd accompany me on personal appearance jobs in nightclubs where we'd get put up in a posh hotel for the night. This sort of supplementary work outside of *Corrie* was often lucrative and I loved being able to spoil him – I bought him designer clothes, I'd give him my card when he went to the pub and I paid all the bills.

As far as I was concerned, I loved him, he was my boyfriend and I wanted to spend my money on him. But young love can be a fickle thing and after about a year of dating, the honeymoon period started to wear off. I'd get a little frustrated with the fact I was paying for everything, including the rent on the apartment we shared. Danny was a lovely guy but didn't seem to have much ambition – I wanted to see some drive from him, but he was quite content to drift.

I spent a fortune on a holiday for the two of us in the

summer of 2009, booking in at a top-notch hotel in Greece, but by the time it came round, I'd had enough. He had a broken leg at the time and my mum felt sorry for him because of that, but I was over the relationship and broke up with him as soon as we got back. I knew he was really gutted which made me feel guilty, but then he sold a story to the *News of the World* about me and that really pissed me off.

He didn't say anything massively horrible, there was no slagging off or settling scores, but he did discuss our sex life and he would have been paid a decent amount of money by the newspaper for that. Grim.

It felt embarrassing more than anything, and a betrayal of trust, but I suppose it confirmed to me that he wasn't The One after all. I'd never want to be with someone capable of doing that. I've actually seen Danny since then and he's an alright guy and there are no hard feelings, but we were never destined for a happily ever after.

After the break-up my mum somehow convinced me to give up the lease on the apartment and come home. I shouldn't have listened to her because I absolutely hated being back there. It's not even like my parents were horrible to me, but there was still a lot of turmoil going on with my brother which led to tensions and arguments and meant the house could be a stressful environment to live in.

It wasn't long before I was plotting my escape route again.

Chapter Four

Spiralling

WITH DANNY OFFICIALLY OFF THE scene, I dated a few guys off and on although they never developed into anything significant. I went out a few times with a Manchester City youth player called Reece Wabara who – and this is *too* funny – Brooke later ended up going out with. We were never serious and I didn't sleep with him but there was one night he took me back to his lodgings after we'd been out in Manchester and his furious landlady kicked me out.

'Er, you're not going upstairs young lady,' she said.

Dead!

Reece was gorgeous but it fizzled out as quickly as it had started and I think he was a bit of a ladies' man anyway. He's actually gone on to have a really successful career away from football with his clothing brand Maniere De Voir which has a flagship store on London's

Oxford Street, so he's come a long way since his landlady was clipping him round the ear for bringing back girls to the house!

Scott Sinclair sidled into my life when I least expected it. I guess that's often the way. When you actively go out looking for love, it's nowhere to be found, almost as if every half-decent man has been snapped up and is off the market with only the losers, idiots and fuckboys left behind.

Love usually happens when you're not looking at all.

It was November 2009 and an ordinary day on the *Corrie* set, nothing to write home about. I was down in the dumps about the latest dreadful character I'd had the misfortune (and appalling judgement) to date, so Brooke suggested that I cheered myself up by coming along with her to the Trafford Centre where she was meeting her friend David for lunch.

I wasn't in the mood for socialising, but I was at a loose end in between scenes and therefore agreed to tag along. Off we went in my green Mini Cooper – my pride and joy at the time – and met David in Nando's where it turned out that he'd brought a friend along with him… Scott.

I'd love to tell you that it was instant fireworks between us and that I knew he was the one for me as soon as our eyes locked, but this isn't Hollywood. This was a rainy day in the middle of a shopping mall in Manchester over a peri-peri chicken. The truth is, I barely noticed Scott let alone fancied him. If anything, I thought he was a bit of a geek.

It was David that I thought was fit because he had a fair bit about him – confidence, quick wit and just the right amount of swagger – very typical of the sort of guy I normally went for but who would inevitably break my heart.

But there was a moment mid-meal when Scott smiled at me and I can still picture it now because I felt myself soften towards him. It was quite a shy smile and suggested that he had a really kind way about him. There was also his West Country accent which was quite unusual to me and when he asked, 'Does anybody want some nuts?' for some reason it made me giggle.

We walked back to the car park and he asked for my BBM number which shows how ancient this story is! In case you're too young to remember, BlackBerry Messenger was an instant messaging system, like a precursor to WhatsApp and everybody was on it.

I wasn't particularly arsed about him, but I thought, 'Oh, Helen, don't be tight!' so I handed my number over, not for one moment thinking anything would come of it. I didn't give it any headspace at all until a couple of days later when he messaged asking how I was and then that started a bit of texting back and forth over the next few weeks.

Scott was a year older than me, a professional footballer on loan at Wigan from Chelsea and I don't think he knew too many people in the area, so when he asked if I wanted to go out sometime, Brooke encouraged me to take him up on the offer.

'Helen,' she said, as we stood in the *Corrie* smoking shelter, puffing away, 'he's a really nice guy. I think he's boyfriend material – you should give him a chance.'

She twisted my arm and so three weeks after we'd first met in Nando's, Scott came to pick me up after work from my parents' house in his Range Rover and took me to this cool French restaurant called Lounge 10 in Manchester where there was a clairvoyant installed in the loo. I know that sounds bonkers, but it was a quirky kind of place and this psychic woman was amazing – she actually once came round to my house when I had a party with my friends and did readings for all of us which proved scarily accurate.

Me and Scott had a gorgeous meal at Lounge 10 where we talked and laughed a lot before moving on to a club. To my surprise, we really hit it off. The chemistry was there without even trying and we vibed off each other in a really natural way.

He was clearly a lovely, soft-hearted guy and different from the other footballers I knew, who could be cocky little arseholes and not particularly nice to women. Scott couldn't have been further from that stereotype and everyone else thought that too – once we were officially dating, I lost count of the number of people who told me, 'Ah, you've got a good one in him.'

From that first date, there was an electric connection between us and we became inseparable, spending every minute we could together. He would come and collect me from work each night and we'd go out for dinner or hang out at his rented flat in Altrincham, which we jokingly used to call 'the prison' because it was all grey and gated.

Despite its nickname, we had such happy times in that apartment, getting to know each other and falling in love, and because I hated staying at my mum's, I moved in quite quickly.

We were a good fit. We came from similar backgrounds and although Scott was a lot quieter than me – I was more outgoing while he was fairly calm – I think we brought out the best in each other. And my mum *loved* him. He had her seal of approval from day one because he's well-spoken and charming and comes across as very mature.

Although on a footballer's wage, Scott wasn't flash with his cash or into designer clothes, he was actually very canny with his money and at the age of just 20 had already invested well. He owned a beautiful penthouse flat near Ascot which we'd go down and stay in if we ever had a couple of days off together and he'd also bought his mum and dad a stunning house in Bath. Over our years as a couple Scott always had an eye out for good property to buy and built up quite the portfolio.

But even though he was a higher earner by some margin, we kept things fairly equal; I had my own money and was always happy to pay my way which felt like the right thing to do. I enjoyed the independence although I thought I was richer than I was.

While Scott was Captain Sensible with his finances, I used to spend my money like water, buying Chanel handbags I really couldn't afford. I didn't have anyone helping me with my money, so I just splurged on whatever I wanted – that would come back to bite me on the backside, believe me.

Scott and I were so young, though. I remember booking a holiday to Dubai and staying at the Jumeirah Burj Al Arab, which had been dubbed the world's first seven-star hotel. Luxurious does not even begin to describe how ridiculously extravagant and OTT this place is and there's me and Scott, this pair of nerds who knew nothing about anything, swanning about all wide-eyed and trying to blend in. Hysterical! We had our own butler for the room, for goodness sake!

We just had the best time together, we made each other so happy and I was in love – properly, madly, crazily in love – for the first time in my life.

But while I did have these pockets of joy with Scott where life seemed easier and I was more comfortable with myself, I'm not going to pretend that the bad stuff magically disappeared. Outside of our relationship, things were pretty bleak and I was struggling with depression while taking a cocktail of meds which, I believe now, were making my situation much worse.

As well as Concerta, I had been put on Roaccutane for my acne, a powerful drug which has since been banned by several countries and is only issued in the UK under strict medical supervision because of its severe side effects and links to depression and suicide ideation. I just felt so dreadfully low, but in my head, I NEEDED these tablets, like I couldn't function without them.

Because the doctor had told me the Concerta would take half an hour to kick in, I took his words completely literally and created a ritual which became a crutch. I'd wake in the morning, have my pill and then have to sit and wait for exactly 30 minutes before I felt able to start my day.

On the surface, I had nothing to be 'depressed' about. I had a great job on *Coronation Street*, a nice boyfriend, loads of friends and people who loved me. But mental health does not discriminate and it was this constant feeling of desperation, hopelessness and an overwhelming sense of doom, like I had a grey cloud hovering ominously over my head. I'd also developed this social anxiety which was becoming crippling and begun to have regular panic attacks. I'd suffered them intermittently over previous years but now they seemed to be happening all the time – wherever, whenever – and they'd come on without warning.

I could be on set at *Corrie*, in coffee shops, in restaurants, at Scott's parents' house – whatever I was doing there was a risk. I'd feel my heart begin to beat really fast,

I'd feel short of breath and break out in a sweat and there was nothing I could do about it.

If I was filming when it started, I'd rush to get to the end of the scene, knowing that within a couple of minutes I was going to be incapable. I'd also started doing this obsessive swallowing routine where I would continually gulp and I was being plagued by tremors in my hands which would shake uncontrollably for, seemingly, no reason.

I hated being at *Corrie*. Trapped in this horrible, negative mindset, I'd come to despise going into work where I felt paranoid that everyone was out to get at me. All I wanted to do was run away and remove myself from everything and I spent a lot of time in my dressing room sobbing but not knowing why I was in such a state.

The actor Antony Cotton, who played Rovers Return barman Sean Tully once reduced me to tears when he took the piss out of the fact I was on medication.

'Here comes Helen Flanagan,' he said. 'You hear her rattling before you see her.'

To him it was a joke for a few cheap laughs, but this was my life. I was just a young girl, struggling to stay afloat and what he said was completely mortifying. I didn't respond, I was too broken. Instead, I went to the toilets and bawled my eyes out.

If someone said something like that to me now, I'd have it out with them. I'd tell them to stop being an insensitive tosser and to fuck right off. I can hold my own with anyone these days, but back then it felt like the end of the world and I cried myself to sleep that night.

I was so embarrassed thinking that must be what everybody thought of me – some bratty little drama queen dosed up on prescription pills in order to function.

It must have been clear that I was finding it all extremely stressful, but no one ever took me aside and tried to get to the bottom of what was going on, not even when I broke down very publicly in January 2010, the day after the National Television Awards in London.

A load of us from *Corrie* had travelled down to the capital for the do where we were up for a ton of awards – I particularly remember this trip because it was coming up to Scott's 21st birthday and I paid a visit to Cartier to buy him a love bracelet.

For the night of the awards, I'd bought myself a blue and gold Alice Temperley dress which I thought was amazing but when I look at pictures now, it makes me think, 'Helen, what the *fuck* were you wearing?!'

I'd also had a criminally dark spray tan and teamed it with some horrific eyelashes which had flecks of gold in them, so I looked like a complete psychopath. All topped off with impossible-to-walk-in gold YSL heels.

A style icon I was not.

Shamefully, a few years later I would manage to outdo even that when I thought it would be a good idea to attend the same awards wearing a pair of sequinned kitten ears and crazy eye make-up which, I'm sure you can imagine, set my D&G dress off a treat. Urgh. I had to go on stage to accept an award for *I'm a Celebrity...Get Me Out of Here* with the goddess that is Ashley Roberts – she was in this elegant white Rachel Gilbert gown while I stood next to her resembling a demented cat.

I honestly despair of myself sometimes.

But back to 2010, when *Corrie* had scooped the coveted Most Popular Serial Drama gong and a couple more besides, and the night had been a lot of fun.

It was the next morning when everything went to shit.

As I was packing up in my hotel room, I checked underneath the bed to make sure I hadn't left anything behind and that's when I saw a man lying there, staring right back at me. I've never been so scared in my life. I screamed and, in the commotion, as I tried to escape the room, I whacked my head on the door full pelt.

I went beserk. I thought someone was trying to kill me.

I made a run for the lift, pressing the buttons repeatedly to try and speed it up, convinced my life was in danger and by the time I got down to reception, I could only collapse on the floor in a shaking heap. Somehow, I managed to get the words out to tell the staff who had surrounded me that there was a man under my bed and the whole hotel was immediately put on lockdown with police called to the scene.

While staff went to investigate the room, I was taken to the manager's office, still trembling with the worst fear I'd ever experienced. It was sheer terror. Katherine Kelly, who played Becky McDonald was there – she's such a lovely, kind person and managed to calm me down while we waited for news.

After about 10 minutes, the manager and security team came into the office and, very gently, told me that there was no strange man under the bed. What *was* there, however, was a discarded mirror and so it turned out that all I'd seen was my own reflection. I didn't believe that was possible, so Katherine took me back into the room and showed me and I had to accept that's what had happened.

She said to reception, 'My friend's OK, she's just not very well.'

Everyone at work thought the whole thing was hilarious and I understood that it must have been funny to them, so I tried to laugh along and give it the old, 'Honestly, what am I like?' act. But inside I was in pieces because I recognised there was something, somewhere going seriously wrong.

I was also ashamed of myself because I'd had the entire hotel running around on a false story. I'm a good person and I'd never intentionally waste anybody's time.

Over the last few years I've tussled with the question of whether the pills I was taking were right for me and I can see now that this was yet another telltale sign about the unsuitability of my medication. That never even crossed my mind at the time and I only wish someone – maybe a producer or some other responsible adult, anyone with a duty of care – had asked exactly what tablets I was on and if I'd thought about the possibility they might be negatively affecting me.

But there was none of that. No one ever brought that up or suggested reviewing what I was putting into my body and it makes me sad to think of now. There might have been an early exit route from the long road of misery that was to come.

The London hotel incident should have sent the alarm bells ringing off the hook. I was taking stimulants from the moment I woke, which I thought was helping my ADHD and my concentration but was actually screwing me up.

I was spiralling and in way over my head.

* * *

When, less than a year into our whirlwind relationship in the summer of 2010, Scott told me that he was being transferred permanently to Swansea, I was devastated, convinced this move more than 200 miles away spelled the end for us. Scott reassured me that he didn't want to break up and we'd make it work – he would travel north whenever his schedule at Swansea allowed and I could come and stay with him at the weekends.

He was so committed and after hearing how determined he was for us to stay together, my heart was full and so began this super cute long-distance relationship. As soon as I finished work for the week, I'd jump in my

Mini and drive down to South Wales, and quite apart from the move breaking us up, it only intensified things between us.

Scott was escapism for me. My family and work lives were increasingly unhappy – things were tumultuous with my brother, and over at *Corrie* I didn't even know if I wanted to be an actress anymore. I'd been doing the job for a decade now, a job I'd taken as a child still in primary school – not many people know what they want to do with the rest of their life at the age of nine. I knew I no longer wanted to be there, but didn't have a clue what I wanted to do instead.

By going down to Swansea where Scott had this beautiful home, and spending time with him in the Mumbles where the coastline is so breathtaking, it was like I could switch off from all the confusion. When I was with him, I felt like I could cope with the mental pain, keep the panic at bay and manage my disordered eating and messed up relationship with food in a much more positive way.

But there were times which were so dire that they started to impact my relationship with Scott – there was one weekend I went to see him and a really bad argument ended in me running into the bathroom and locking the door.

I was trying to hurt myself and poor Scott was freaking out. He had no experience of anything like this, there had been no mental health challenges in his family or close circle, so it was completely alien to him. His attitude then (and, if I'm being honest, throughout our relationship) tended to be along the lines of 'get over it and get on with it'.

By the end of 2010 I had sunk even further into a depression and was aching to leave *Corrie*, knowing that staying there wasn't doing me any good. Quite the opposite actually. It had become detrimental to my mental wellbeing and I longed to go somewhere I could live a quieter, more normal life and try to get my health back on track.

But I was contracted for another 12 months and didn't think there was a cat in hell's chance of me being released from it. The only person who really got a hold of the situation was Alison Sinclair, our legendary head of press – she's been there for decades and so knows everyone really well.

I went into work one day in February 2011 and must have looked in a right mess because Alison clocked me and said, 'Oh my God, Helen, I'm so sorry and don't take this the wrong way, but you look absolutely awful. As a mum, I can't watch this, we need to do something.'

I instantly broke down in tears and told Alison I wanted to leave, I needed to get out, but couldn't because I was under contract.

'Don't you worry about that,' she said. 'We'll get you out of that contract. You're a young girl and this isn't right. You can't carry on like this.'

Alison, God love her, went out on a limb for me and headed straight to see producer Kieran Roberts, telling him he needed to let me go and allow me to get well.

No ifs, no buts.

We were bang in the middle of filming, but after his conversation with Alison, Kieran spoke to the storyliners about getting me written out of the script as quickly as possible.

The press were told I was taking a three-month sabbatical to spend more time with Scott and that's how it was reported, but I was actually signed off on a mental health note.

After 11 years, I was leaving *Coronation Street*. And I couldn't wait to say goodbye.

Chapter Five

Freedom

THE FIRST THING I DID when I walked away from the cobbles was cut off all my hair and dye it peroxide blonde. A teeny bit dramatic? Guilty as charged.

You might want to call it an early mid-life crisis because like a total cliché I also went out and bought a Range Rover on finance which I definitely couldn't afford and rented myself a luxury apartment in Alderley Edge. Which, ditto.

These were all big, bold moves and fairly out of character, but together it was as if I was making a statement, trying to reclaim my life and take some sort of charge of it. Everything was now on my terms although I was living in cloud-cuckoo-land if I thought that I was going to be able to sustain it.

I also took a long holiday to Florida with Scott – we were closer than ever during that time – and having the warmth of sun on my face as we ate breakfast together outside felt like freedom. I'd been released into the wild and was able to breathe again.

Those three months off work weren't without their difficulties. I wasn't miraculously 'cured' and I was still relying on medication to get me through each day, but minus the added pressure of being on *Corrie* and in the media, life felt calmer and my panic attacks became much less frequent.

Not having to be on telly three times a week meant I didn't fret half as much about how I looked and the press interest scaled right back, leaving me able to go about my business without being papped. I started to feel genuinely comfortable in my own skin again.

I kept myself entertained by doing not very much at all. I'd worked since the age of nine (and even before that if you count the commercials I'd appeared in) so I'd never experienced being footloose and fancy free. I was long overdue this break.

I also absolutely *loved* my new pixie crop which I'd copied from a model I'd seen in a magazine. It was such a different look for me and marked a clear separation between me and Rosie Webster which I reckon was psychologically important. Having grown up as this character, the lines between me and her had often become blurred in my head and I needed to find my own identity as Helen.

Not everyone was quite as enamoured with the hair,

though. After my sabbatical was over but before I returned to *Corrie* full-time, I was due to film a three-part spin-off series called *Just Rosie* for ITV.com and when the producer Phil Collinson caught wind of the hair 'situation', he gave me hell for messing everything up.

I no longer looked like Rosie Webster which was a problem for him – a huge one – and he was absolutely furious with me. He said there was no way Rosie would have undergone a cut so severe, she was far too vain and conscious of her looks to make such a drastic change and that the only way to salvage this disaster was for me to agree to dye it back brown.

I was crushed. I adored the peroxide, I thought it looked wicked. But it also symbolised something far greater to me – my new beginning, my reset. I begged Phil not to make me do that.

He wouldn't hear of it and marched me up to the head of make-up who was lovely with me but said she'd been told there was no room for negotiation on this. My hair had to be dyed back.

I accepted my fate but was gutted with the results. Gone was the super cool blonde crop and in its place was something that looked not unlike a toilet brush. I looked hideous!

They'd dealt with the situation so heavy-handedly – I was a 21-year-old girl returning to work for the first time after a mental health breakdown so a bit of sensitivity wouldn't have gone amiss.

If he'd said, 'Helen, I understand that things are difficult for you just now, but you need to check with hair and make-up before you do anything to alter your look,' I would have responded a lot better.

I really didn't want to do this spin-off show. Despite the time off, I still wasn't in the right frame of mind for it and being back on set reignited the familiar negative thought processes. *Just Rosie* was a comedy and supposed to gently take the piss out of Rosie, who had become a bit of a caricature and was attempting to break into the modelling industry in London. Her various escapades across the three episodes would throw up funny scenarios like her thinking she'd landed a top job which turned out to be a promotional gig and having to dress in a monkey suit.

But I took everything so personally and assumed I was being stitched up by the writers and producers to look like a complete idiot.

'How can we make Helen look as moronic as possible today?'

That's what I thought they were conspiring to do.

I can see now that *Just Rosie* was actually a cute little series and it was testament to the character (and, I suppose, me) that she'd been given her own show, but back then I couldn't see past the idea that everyone was out to get at me.

To this day, I've still not watched it and think I would struggle to do so even now all these years later because it would remind me of how dismal I felt at the time.

And I totally hold my hands up to the fact that all of this meant I could be, let's say, 'hard work' and there were moments during filming where it all got too much and I'd just walk off set and drive myself to Starbucks.

I was on 18mg of Concerta – a slow-release stimulant – three times a day. I've since discovered it's only recommended to be taken as a single tablet once daily so no wonder it was making me paranoid and irrational where I'd be having these private meltdowns in my dressing room thinking I was the butt of everyone's joke. Again, some of that came back to the hazy boundaries between me and Rosie so I'd almost get offended on her behalf.

Once we'd finished filming *Just Rosie*, I immediately returned to the main show, and things picked up where we'd left off with Rosie as the resident temptress, and one of the storylines involved her seducing her mother Sally's boyfriend, Jeff.

We filmed those scenes in the Midland Hotel in Manchester and it was a day when I was particularly wrecked with depression; my skin had broken out, I had my horrible toilet brush hair and they'd dressed me in a diamante lilac bra and a really short skirt.

The actor who played Jeff was a much older man and although he couldn't have been nicer, I was nervous and uncomfortable about filming this bedroom scene. Just before the cameras started rolling, the director said something to me which left me reeling. He whispered in my ear, almost matter-of-factly, 'Just look at him as if you want to fuck him.'

It felt like a punch to the stomach. I didn't know how to respond to that, it was like a violation. This director was an older man in a position of power and to speak to me like that was shocking and I quickly became inconsolably upset.

Most of the crew were just like, 'Oh, Helen's off again, acting like the diva.'

In my head I've replayed that exchange over and over and I've thought of hundreds of ways I should have come back at him using the feistiness I've acquired now with age, experience and healing. In my favourite alternative version, I reply, 'Don't ever talk to me like that again. How fucking dare you?'

But I was young and in a vulnerable place, and the only response I could muster was to dissolve into tears.

I think that was the point I knew I had to get out permanently.

I just wasn't a happy girl at all. I was a lost soul. And I know that people called me 'hard work Helen' or 'mad Helen' and to anyone who wasn't aware of what was going on, I get why they'd see me as that. It was a crying shame that I was in such a bad way because I had such an incredible job and so many amazing opportunities right at my feet.

But my heart just wasn't in it anymore. And my head? My head was all over the bloody shop.

HEAD & HEART

* * *

Sally Dynevor was the first person I told of my plan to quit for real and she thought I'd lost my mind. She couldn't understand my decision at all.

'But Helen,' she said, 'what are you going to do?'

'I don't know,' I replied. 'I just know I can't stay here.'

I knew she was coming at it from a place of concern because she loved and cared about me, but she obviously thought I was chucking my life away and she tried everything she could to talk me out of it. But once I'd made my decision to leave, I remained very single-minded and strong about it and nothing was going sway me back.

There was this immense sense of relief, like a weight off my chest, knowing I was going to be walking away for good and would be able to get on with my life. I didn't know what the future held and I didn't have any alternative career or revenue streams lined up, but I didn't care. All that mattered was I could wake up in the morning in charge of my own destiny and with a clear(er) head.

It also meant I would be able to spend more time in Swansea with Scott – our relationship was the best thing about my life and he was over the moon that we were going to get to be together the whole time. I was so excited that I was going to be cocooned in what was my only safe space.

Sally wasn't the only one who thought I was making a mistake. So many people would ask what I was planning on doing and when I told them that I genuinely didn't know, they'd look at me as if I'd gone doolally.

There was one really nice director lady and when I told her that the only thing I was sure about was moving to Swansea to live with my boyfriend, she said, 'Aw, that's really romantic!'

It was the first positive reaction I'd received and I thought to myself, yes it *is* romantic! I only wished more people could see that this was a decision I'd taken for myself and my health – as far as I was concerned, it wasn't just the best thing I could do, it was the *only* thing.

I also had a conversation about it in the toilets with Michelle Keegan, and when I told her that I had no plans apart from moving in with Scott and she said, 'Oh, I really want what you and Scott have got. He loves you, and you love him, you're lucky to have each other. I wish I had that.'

It's hard to believe that someone like Michelle could ever have been unlucky in love and I'm so glad she later found her own fairytale with Mark Wright.

I didn't want to discuss my decision with the producer I had nicknamed Voldemort, so instead I broke the news to Kieran Roberts who I'd always felt more supported by and he listened and understood my reasons and agreed to write me out. And I was pleased when they told me that they weren't going to kill Rosie off – death is the worst possible way for a soap actor to leave a show because it closes the door to any chance of a return, although at that point I had no intention of ever coming back.

My exit storyline saw Rosie being offered a part on a reality TV series and moving to London, giving her the fame she'd always craved (careful what you wish for Rosie, love). Her big break meant she'd have to end things with boyfriend Jason Grimshaw because being single was a prerequisite for the reality show and in typically ruthless fashion, she broke his heart.

Me and Ryan Thomas, who played Jason, weren't on the best of terms in real life either – we used to clash something chronic, mainly because he would be dead grumpy in the mornings and never used to know his lines! I probably needed to lighten up a little bit, but he once told me outright that he didn't like me and I told him to fuck off (mature of me). Over the years since, however, we've moved in similar circles and become quite good friends and I've got a lot of time for Ryan and his brothers, Adam and Scott. They're good lads.

I filmed my final scenes at the turn of 2012 and that was it. Goodbye, Rosie Webster.

Ta-ra, chuck.

I quit, convinced this was the solution, the magic pill to all my woes. And in some ways it was. For a little while, anyway. But, I was about to learn that mental health issues don't just disappear and life was still more than capable of throwing me great giant curveballs.

I was out of the chip pan and into the fryer.

When I say I didn't have a plan after leaving *Coronation Street*, that's not strictly true.

I did have an ambition I wanted to fulfil and that was to go to drama school. Besides Carol Godby's classes and the learning I'd done on the job, I'd never had any formal acting training and I got it into my head that I'd like to study the craft and sharpen my skills as an actress.

There was a noticeable difference between the actors on *Corrie* who had been to drama school and those who hadn't. Please no one take that as an insult, because I don't necessarily mean in terms of ability or strength. It was more a confidence thing and hard to put your finger on because it was fairly subtle, but I loved watching people like Katherine Kelly, who had trained at the prestigious Royal Academy of Dramatic Art. I found it quite mesmerising seeing how they carried themselves and put all that top class teaching into practice.

Part of me also felt like I'd missed out on the uni experience my school friends had enjoyed while I was out working – going to drama school would be a way to recover a bit of that, albeit belatedly.

And so I decided that I wanted to audition for RADA. I was deadly serious.

Before I left *The Street*, I'd confided in Katherine about my hopes to win a place there and she was so encouraging. Plus, I'd always wanted to live in London so it felt like the perfect fit for me.

I wasn't daft enough to think I could waltz straight into an audition and be handed a place – I knew it was going to take a fair bit of prep, which I was happy to do and, of course, I now had the time to put the work in.

As an early 22nd birthday present, Scott paid for some acting lessons with an ex-drama teacher from RADA and she coached me specifically for the audition. We did some intensive drama sessions as well as singing lessons and in the summer I headed down to London for my audition, determined that this was going to be the start of my new chapter and a future I could look forward to.

Only it didn't quite go to plan.

I think I'd built it up into something way too big and so when I didn't get through the first round, it was a shock to me. I had truly thought the piece I'd prepared – a monologue and a song – was really strong and that I had a good chance of sailing through. But it wasn't to be and I was back at square one.

Had I been kidding myself? Did this mean my acting career was over? If I wasn't deemed good enough for RADA, did I have any hope of continuing to work in the industry? I was so disappointed because by then I'd had my heart set on it and the rejection felt like a smack in the gob.

I tried to focus on the many things I had to be grateful for. Scott had just been transferred to Manchester City so we moved back north and set up home together in a beautiful house in Prestbury, a village in Cheshire where lots of footballers and their families lived. We'd also enjoyed a holiday to the Maldives that summer which is the sort of destination dreams are made of – I had much to be thankful for.

Maybe RADA just hadn't been meant for me. I told myself that perhaps that particular door closing was going to set me on another path.

Well, it certainly did that...

Remember I told you earlier that I used to spend like there was no tomorrow? I didn't have a grip on my finances at all, partly because I was so bloody dopey, but also because no one had ever shown me how to. I didn't have an accountant or financial advisor and all my parents' energy went towards keeping my dad's business going.

Again, it was a case of on the surface, everything looking fine. I'd had a good job, was settled in a nice relationship and appeared to be getting along in life so they didn't see any need to interfere. But I hadn't had an agent since I was 16 and so my *Corrie* wages hadn't increased in the five years until I left because there was no one negotiating for me. I can't actually believe now that I was in that position.

I had full access to my bank account but no concept of money, budgeting or savings. I had no idea how much I was getting paid or what my balance was. I'd buy a pair of Louboutins and then tell myself I might as well get the matching handbag, too. I'd wander into Selfridge's for a browse and come out with a Chanel without a second thought. It was reckless behaviour where I spent whatever I wanted… until one day I couldn't.

I was in Tesco doing the weekly food shop and this was a few days after I'd splashed out on a Prada handbag and a Valentino dress from Flannels. When I went to pay for the items in my trolley, my card was declined.

I couldn't understand what was wrong and so went over to use the cashpoint to try and get some money that way, but it refused to pay out. On the screen it was showing I had literally nothing left in my account.

What. The. Hell.

I had no choice but to leave all the shopping behind in the store and drive home empty-handed to tell Scott what had happened. And if I was expecting sympathy from him, I didn't get any. Scott blew up.

'Are you fucking joking, Helen? Where's all your money gone?'

'I don't know… I've just spent it all.'

We had this huge row because Scott, who had always been so cautious and clever with money, could not wrap his head around the fact I'd been so careless. And I was upset seeing him so cross with me – he'd never been as angry.

I was also mad with myself for ballsing it up so badly and I just thought, 'Oh, my fucking god, what am I going to do?'

Obviously I knew I wasn't going to be destitute or on

the streets because Scott was a footballer on a Premiership wage, and he, very generously, gave me some money to tide me over while I sorted myself out.

But I'd always prided myself on being able to contribute to the relationship financially and paying my own way. I know I used to say that I wanted to be a WAG when I grew up, but I'd come to value my independence and being able to support myself. I didn't want to live off Scott's money, I was only 22 and capable of earning my own.

I knew I had to get my act together and start bringing in some money again, so I quickly found myself an agent and started getting some bits of work here and there. I did some modelling jobs and a couple of magazine shoots which brought in a decent whack.

But then came the hammer blow. I'd thought having my card declined in Tesco was humiliating enough but being presented with a tax bill I didn't have a hope in hell of paying was the kicker. I was physically sick when I saw the five-figure sum I owed HMRC and I know now that I should have been putting money aside to cover it but, like I say, I was completely ignorant.

So that unholy mess of a tax bill is precisely how I ended up getting down and dirty with the cockroaches and witchety grubs on *I'm a Celebrity Get Me Out of Here...!*

And in a whole lot more hot water than I could ever have imagined.

Chapter Six

Get Me Out of Here

WHEN I SIGNED ON THE dotted line to join the 2012 series of *I'm a Celebrity…!*, I had zero idea what I was letting myself in for. I went into this thing completely blind, knowing virtually nothing about the show.

Now, I appreciate that might sound like a bizarre thing to say, not least because it's consistently been one of ITV's most-watched programmes since it began way back in 2002. But I never used to spend much of my spare time watching TV – after working in that industry all day with *Corrie*, it was usually the last thing I wanted to sit and 'do' when I got home.

The only real knowledge I had of what went on in the jungle was from the legendary Katie Price and Peter Andre season of 2004 because their romance had been so highly-publicised during the run and, of course, for many years beyond it.

In my mind, the basic premise was a load of dead nice people with interesting lives bonding around a campfire while getting fabulous tans. That seemed right up my street.

What could possibly go wrong?

Everyone tried to talk me out of it. Over dinner my mum said, 'Helen, you don't understand – this show is not for you… it's not too late to pull out.'

I hadn't dared to reveal to Mum the extent of my financial difficulties, so she didn't realise it was more a case of *needing* to do it rather than wanting to. Given the fact I had this tax bill and no money to pay it with, I had no choice.

Scott was dead against it, too.

'If you do it, I'm not even going to watch it,' he said. 'I swear to God, I can't sit and watch you in that jungle.'

I don't even know why he was so mardy about it, but it's obvious now that his, let's say, 'unsupportive' attitude was a sign that things were starting to get a bit wonky between the two of us. I loved Scott with every fibre of my soul and I knew he loved me too, but he'd developed a bit of a nasty side, one I never understood.

He was struggling with his football career, finding the pressures of breaking into the first team at Man City extremely tough and there were occasions when he took those frustrations out on me. He was never, ever aggressive or physically intimidating – I have to be clear about that – but he could be vicious with his tongue and he knew exactly how to hurt me.

Now, I know what you might be thinking. If Scott was so averse to me doing *I'm a Celebrity...!*, why didn't he just pay off my tax bill? As a Premiership footballer, he was earning more than enough to support the two of us and he could have cleared my debts in one fell swoop with barely a dent to his wallet, saving me a lot of pain in the process.

The simple answer is that he didn't offer and I would never have asked him. To be fair, he'd bailed me out in the past and he probably (quite rightly) thought this wasn't his responsibility. We weren't married, we didn't have kids together and this was a mess I'd managed to create all on my own, so it figured that it was also mine to mop up. I was an adult and needed to stand on my own two feet.

Therefore, in November 2012 I flew out to Australia, still oblivious to the horrors awaiting, although the reality started to dawn on me when I was told I had to enter the camp via a makeshift, wobbly bridge which stretched across a 200ft ravine.

FML.

I froze with fear. I couldn't move. All the colour drained from my face and I thought I was going to be sick. My teammates David Haye, Linda Robson, Brian Conley and Charlie Brooks all strode across without too much fuss, but even though I was attached to a harness and there was zero chance of me plunging to a grisly death, no amount of coaxing and pep-talking from the crew made the blindest bit of difference. In the end – and this was never shown on camera – they had to have someone physically push me across because it was getting dark and they were losing the light to shoot.

So, I was already a nervous wreck when I arrived in the camp and, I kid you not, the first thing I noticed was that there were rats *everywhere*. I'd never seen a live rat before and I was absolutely beside myself – they were scuttling past our feet, having a great time gallivanting around the campfire and seemed to be wherever I turned. And while I'm certain they weren't dangerous (I believe now they were actually set rats planted by production) I was absolutely horrified, and not for the first time that day, thought I might just have made a terrible mistake in coming here.

For the first few days, we were split between two camps – Croc Creek and Snake Rock – and went head-to-head with each other in the bushtucker trials to win stars (which converted to meals) for our respective teams. Little did I know that my tearful ordeal on the bridge was going to put me in the line of fire when the public came to vote for which celebs they wanted to take part in the trials. Apparently viewers like to see people suffering...

Presenters Ant and Dec announced that the audience at home had selected me from Croc Creek and the then Tory MP Nadine Dorries from Snake Rock to compete in the first trial which they'd ominously named Bug Burial.

The deal was that me and Nadine each had to lie in a closed coffin lowered into the ground while they added spiders, snakes, bugs, rats and all manner of other disgusting jungle creatures to join us. We had to remain locked in there for 10 minutes to win the maximum number of stars for camp.

I couldn't bear it. I lasted a grand total of four seconds before saying, 'I'm a celebrity, get me out of here!' and it was game over for me.

Nadine managed about four minutes before doing the same and so we both went back to our camps with no stars and therefore no meals. At that point I couldn't see myself lasting another 24 hours and, hilariously, the producers caught me on camera saying I wanted to 'call my agent' to get me out!

I genuinely had no idea it would be this bad.

Thankfully, my Croc Creek campmates were really supportive and I consoled myself with the naive thought that having been so useless at the first trial, no one would bother voting for me to do another one.

What I hadn't banked on was the public finding all this quite entertaining. People at home had rather enjoyed watching me perform so abysmally and then seeing the other celebs go hungry as a result.

And so when Ant and Dec returned the next day to announce the two celebs who had been voted to compete in 'Rotten Rhymes', it was myself and Nadine again. This time it was an eating trial – each dish was worth one meal, but only the winning celebrity could take those meals back to their camp.

I passed on the first offering which was a giant baked spider (gross). I attempted the camel's toe before spitting it out (I have no words to describe how disgusting this was) but – yay, me! – I did manage to eat the fermented duck egg.

After three rounds, it was 2-1 to Nadine.

With a lot of gagging, both of us somehow chomped our way through the ostrich anus (literally the worst thing I've ever put in my mouth) but we each drew the line at the lamb's testicles in the final round.

No thanks.

It meant that Nadine won the trial 3-2 and I was returning to Croc Creek empty-handed again, but I was proud of myself for getting through the trial and trying my best.

I'd just eaten an ostrich's arsehole, FFS!

Unfortunately, I don't think my fellow campmates, who were famished after two days on basic rations of rice and beans, saw it in quite the same way. Anyone who thinks the hunger is all for show, and that producers secretly keep the celebrities fed, is sorely mistaken. No stars equals no food and we were genuinely starving in there.

On the third day, the two camps merged making us one big dysfunctional jungle family and I felt sure that with a much bigger pool of celebs to choose from, my time being voted to do the trials was over.

Wrong.

When Ant and Dec entered camp to reveal that it

would be yours truly facing some sadistic horror show called 'Cruelty Towers' I could have cried. I was scared witless of these flipping trials.

The hunger was undoubtedly heightening my panic and the result was this vicious circle because the anxiety was making it impossible for me to perform in the trials and without the stars, there was nothing to eat. In addition to that, I was still on the ADHD meds every day which you're not supposed to take without food and so that was causing an extreme reaction which was only putting me further on edge.

I was effectively on speed while doing these trials and everyone was sitting at home going, 'We hate that girl, shall we make her do another one?!'

And I can see it must have been funny for people watching but, for me, it was next-level awful and also a form of self-sabotage because the worse I performed at the trials, the more likely I was to be voted to go again the following day.

Cruelty Towers, my third trial, was set up to resemble a hotel and the mission was to go through various rooms which were filled with unspeakable grossness to collect the stars.

I steeled myself.

Come on, Helen. Focus. A few minutes and you'll be done.

I entered the first room where I was confronted with a live bloody ostrich in a confined space. I tried to stay calm. But what I hadn't registered was that as soon as I removed the lightbulb to get the first star, it would plunge the whole set into darkness. It was pitch black and I freaked out.

I couldn't do it.

'I'm a celebrity, get me out of here!'

I could hear the collective sigh of exasperation from the crew.

Again, I had to return to camp and break the news to everyone that, thanks to me, we were going hungry again. People like Linda Robson were very kind about it – she was soft as anything and told me not to worry.

David Haye was always really supportive although I now think he probably had an ulterior motive for that. I'd first seen David when we'd all stayed in this fancy villa before heading into the camp and I'd thought he was absolutely beautiful. From the beginning I loved being around him.

I could tell he liked me – he made that much obvious – but I was with Scott, and David was married at the time with two young children which meant we were both off limits and I'd never have done anything to jeopardise our relationships on the outside. Nevertheless, he used to try and wind me up in the camp, saying silly things like, 'Do you *really* think that Scott's never cheated on you?' and Charlie Brooks would tell him to drop it.

'She's just a young girl, leave her alone,' she'd say.

He'd also tell me to think of all the deals that would

be waiting for me when I got out which I thought was a bit weird, him taking such an interest in my career. But I was also flattered that this gorgeous guy was paying me this much attention and was a bit gutted when the two camps merged and the former Pussycat Doll Ashley Roberts joined us because I knew she was going to catch his eye.

'Oh well, that's my fun over!' I thought.

But David didn't let up on the flirtiness and it carried on after we left the jungle with phone calls and DMs which started to become a bit much. He phoned me once after an arty topless shot I'd done for my calendar found its way into the papers.

'Why did you do that, babe?' he asked, disappointed in me. 'If you needed the money, I would have given it to you.'

Slightly odd.

I eventually blocked him after he sent me a video which I thought was inappropriate. I knew it was supposed to be funny, but I found it unsettling and so I decided to put a stop to all contact.

It would be nearly a decade before me and David Haye crossed paths again and this time, he would turn my world upside down. But more on that later.

* * *

The next *I'm a Celebrity...!* trial was Come Dive With Me, and, surprise surprise, it was me again. Only, this one was another double-header and I was up with Charlie Brooks. We had to get into a tank with actual crocodiles and dive under the water to retrieve the stars with our teeth.

I mean, who even comes up with these demonic ideas?

I'd been in too much of a tizz at the start to listen to the instructions properly and used my hands rather than my teeth to get the stars, so even though I came out with four, every single one of them was disqualified. On the plus side, Charlie had bagged quite a few, so at least we were going to have some food for camp which wasn't the rice and beans we were all now heartily sick of.

On our walk back to camp, Charlie, who had already made it obvious that her patience with me was running out, told me that she thought I over-dramatised and her comments stung a little because that's not what I was doing – all my reactions were completely real. I wasn't performing for the cameras.

I know there were people watching who thought my meltdowns had all been part of some cunning game plan for airtime. Er, no. Why would I want to go on TV and humiliate myself like that? The better strategy would have been to go in there like a boss bitch, nail every trial and emerge as a hero and probably queen of the jungle, too.

I can assure you, there was no game plan.

Of course I didn't want to look like a loser! But I also knew that if I quit the show, then according to the terms of my contract, I wasn't getting paid and that nightmarish tax bill wouldn't be going anywhere.

By my fifth consecutive trial, I was spent. I didn't have the energy or mental strength to do it and despite Ant and Dec trying to talk me into starting Rodent Run which would see me on a giant hamster wheel while god knows what was tipped over my head, I just couldn't find it in myself.

Every time I stepped on the wheel to start the trial, a wave of anxiety would come over me and I'd have to get off again. After several false starts I called time on the whole thing and refused to do it.

Even Ant and Dec were pissed off with me now. Dec was always quite sweet but Ant made no attempt to disguise his frustration. And, you know what? I got it. A lot of time, effort and money is spent on getting the trials ready and so to have someone not even attempt it must have been infuriating.

Surely the joke for the audience at home must have been wearing thin, too? Well, apparently not because the next day I was voted to do my SIXTH trial in a row.

This time, my campmates ditched the tea and sympathy and gave me some tough love. Hugo Taylor was one of my best mates in there – I'm sure he thought I was totally precious, but he also recognised a girl who was completely out of her depth – but even he didn't pull any punches now.

'Look, Helen,' he said before I headed off to face the

trial, 'if you don't smash this, everyone is going to be really angry with you… you have to come back with some stars, no excuses.'

I was under no illusions about how much depended on me delivering the goods with this one.

The trial was called Deadly Delivery and I had to manoeuvre a star through a maze with my hands while my head was in a Perspex box filled with lizards, cockroaches and pythons.

It was revolting and stressful, but in an astonishing turnaround of events and to the surprise of everyone (and especially myself) I won 12 out of 12 stars! Buzzing!

If I'm being completely honest, I think the team behind the scenes deliberately made it easier for me, knowing the camp was starving and that I was at breaking point. I don't want to take anything away from the personal achievement, but the crew stayed really close to me the whole time out of camera shot and I could see the doctor and psychologist there which was reassuring – it didn't feel anything like as scary as the previous trials.

Whether they helped me out or not, the triumph and relief of going back to camp to tell the others they'd finally be having a decent meal that evening put me on top of the world.

And despite the bushtucker trials misery, I did have some great days in the jungle and I can look back on my time there now and laugh at how ridiculous I was. Like the fact I took in fake tan as my luxury item, slapped about a gallon of it on without a care in the world and then looked like an Oompa Loompa for the next several days.

I have no regrets about my time there. I might not have covered myself in glory with the trials, but I was never unkind to anyone. It takes a lot for me to dislike someone, so I got along with my campmates on the whole. What they thought of me is another matter…

However, there's no way I should have passed the psyche test to be on it. Producers knew I'd been signed off from *Coronation Street* on mental health grounds and that I relied on medication to get through the day. I also remember telling the series psychologist that my relationship with Scott was quite turbulent because this was around the time he'd begun to be a little bit mean.

And yet they still passed me as fit and well to go on. In the years since, we've all seen how reality TV controversies (and tragedies) have forced production companies and the networks to buck their ideas up when it comes to their duty of care, and I don't think it would happen now. Applying the standards of today, I'm pretty sure I wouldn't have been let within a country mile of that show.

In the end, I was the fifth celeb to be eliminated and I was happy to walk out of there although the most insane thing of all was that I'd actually started off thinking I was going to win! I was clearly deluded beyond all reason, but I knew I was a nice girl and I'd thought people would like me. I had no clue that the whole country absolutely hated me until I came out, saw all the negative press and just went, 'Oh my god, what the hell happened here?'

* * *

I liked Charlie Brooks and thought she was a kick-ass kind of woman, but I 100 percent know I got on her nerves. At certain points she didn't even try to hide her disdain for me. There was a really funny incident when we'd been sitting around the campfire and something dropped on my shoulder making me jump out of my skin. I'd thought it was a snake or a massive spider, but it turned out to be only a leaf and Charlie's eyes just about rolled out the back of her head at my reaction.

I'm sure she found me tedious and I know she was fuming with me a lot of the time because she was so hungry. But when she was crowned queen of the jungle, she did something on the ITV2 spin-off show which even one of the producers told me was unfair. It really upset my mum, too.

All the campmates were there and everyone was really happy for Charlie – she had deserved to win, no doubt – but when she was asked if there were any negatives to her jungle experience, she didn't miss a beat and said, 'Helen!'

My heart dropped.

'I wish she'd tried harder in the trials,' she said. 'She didn't do enough.'

Wow. That was a bit savage. We were live on telly so I had to sit there and pretend to smile along. This was supposed to be a celebration of the series and her victory, not a time to have personal digs or settle scores. Could she not have enjoyed the fact she'd won and left me alone? There was no need especially because I was already dealing with being branded 'the most hated *I'm a Celebrity...* contestant ever' which was as hurtful as it was baffling to me. I'd not fallen out with anyone or behaved like a cow, I was just shit at the trials. It seemed like such an extreme reaction to something so minor, and I couldn't get my head around being this reviled, but the media really went to town on me and it carried on for weeks, long after the series ended.

I was rattled about the fact that people were commenting on and questioning my character, and it was Helen they hated, not Rosie, which was new territory for me and, obviously, incredibly personal.

My mum was horrified by all the terrible press and seeing her getting in such a flap about it made my anxiety worse and I couldn't stand the drama of it all. As far as the media were concerned, I was their new villain and they were not going to give me any leeway.

It's really hard for me to go back and think about that time because everything got quite dark for a while and it all built up to one of the worst moments of my life.

On December 17th, just days after returning from the jungle, I posted a picture on Twitter from a shoot

I'd done a few months before which showed me in a black bra and holding a gun to my temple. I captioned it, 'Head fuck' in reference to a hangover I was suffering that day.

I didn't give it a second thought, but what I hadn't realised because I was in my own little world, was that this was the same day as the first funerals of the Sandy Hook shooting victims in Connecticut. Twenty-six people including 20 children aged six and seven had been killed by a crazed gunman three days earlier.

I'd seen the news of the attack, but hadn't been aware of the funerals and, stupidly, I didn't make the link between the story and my photo. Although it was very silly of me, it was innocently done and as soon as I received a tweet telling me I needed to take down the picture, I was mortified and deleted it. I immediately understood the implication and that I needed to be much more careful about what I was posting.

But the next day it was splashed across the front page of *the Sun* with the headline, 'Brainless: how could you, Helen?'

Words can't describe how awful I felt in that moment. I wanted to die. I'd had many different kinds of low in my life, but waking up to see that front page was the lowest.

It prompted a Twitter storm and I've never known anything as ferocious. I had people telling me to go and kill myself and what an horrendous person I was and the situation quickly spun out of control. I was at the centre of this pile-on, a relentless barrage of abuse and death threats which I didn't know how to stop.

OK, the picture was tone deaf and offensive. One million percent. To this day I regret it wholeheartedly and I can't begin to imagine what those children and their parents suffered. But there was not an ounce of malice attached to what I did. I'm someone who would lay down their life for any child.

In the days that followed, I was advised (badly, I now believe) to go on *Daybreak* which was ITV's breakfast show at the time, to talk about it and issue an apology. I needed to find some way of drawing a line under it and getting the outrage on social media to quieten down. I was also losing work from the fallout having been dropped from an upcoming episode of *Who Wants to be a Millionaire?*.

I shouldn't have gone on *Daybreak*. I'd never had any media training, I was still extremely upset and not strong enough to withstand a grilling on a live TV news show. This was an ongoing situation and I was like a rabbit caught in the headlights, being put through the wringer for the benefit of a nation baying for my blood. Instead of clearing everything up, the interview threw fuel on the fire and gave fresh legs to the story, giving rise to another wave of threats and abuse.

If I'd been in a financial position where I could have run away and never shown my face again, I would have dropped everything and taken that option. I seriously thought about killing myself. I just didn't want to be here because it felt like my brain couldn't take the hate which was being slung in my direction.

The Christmas and New Year holiday gave me a chance to lie low for a while and I actively stayed out of the spotlight to allow myself to recover, and for the vitriol to die down. Which it did, eventually, as people moved on to the next controversy to get hopping mad about, but I was overwhelmed with shame for a long time afterwards.

I learned a valuable lesson from the whole experience and I never post anything now without checking and double-checking there's nothing in the news which is going to clash and cause an issue. I probably do my friends' heads in asking them to give me the all-clear on everything because it's often hard to trust my own judgment. But I can also see that I wasted a lot of energy worrying about something that was a stupid mistake and certainly didn't make me a bad person.

Making that stormy period even more challenging was the fact that me and Scott were, by now, going through what I would call a rocky patch. He was still smarting over the fact I'd done *I'm a Celebrity…!* against his wishes and things were tough for him footballing-wise, so all in all, we weren't in a great place.

We'd gone to the Man City Christmas party together which I'd been looking forward to because I got on with the other girls there and the two of us were papped on the way in. As soon as Scott saw the photographer, he let go of my hand which was confusing and he was then in a vile mood all night.

At one point he came back from the bar and I said, 'Oh, babe, have you got me a drink?'

'Get your own fucking drink,' he replied, out of nowhere, in front of the other players and their partners which was so demeaning – I have no idea why he behaved like that, because I adored him.

When we got back to our house later that night, we had the mother of all rows, almost chasing each other around the bed, screaming.

'How dare you humiliate me in front of everyone?' I said, through tears of rage.

I never knew what would trigger this nastiness in him, but it had started to come out a lot, and there was another time at a family dinner when he'd made fun of me incessantly, saying that I was a 'bimbo' and 'thick' in front of all of his relatives.

Another time on a night out at a posh hotel which had plush padded walls, he'd said to our friends, 'The padded walls are for Helen because she's fucking mental.'

It was constant digs, like he was chipping away at me – he had the ability to make me feel tiny and worthless.

And yet I loved him to death! Scott was my safety blanket and even when he was being horrible, I'd rather have been with him than with anyone else. I'd tried to leave him once, though, before I went into the jungle when he wasn't being very nice to me. But my mum had told me to try couples counselling.

'But, Mum,' I said, 'I'm not happy, I've had enough of him.'

It'sShe wouldn't hear of it, so I was more than a little bit stuck. If, when she's older, my daughters come to me and say, 'Mum, this guy's being a prick to me' I'd take them straight in and get them away from him. That's my mentality as a mother. I'd be so fierce.

By the time everything came to a head with me and Scott in the spring of 2013, our relationship had been falling apart for several months. It was early May and I had booked myself in for a nose job in Greece. It was my first foray into cosmetic surgery (although it wouldn't be my last) and I thought it would be the answer to the deep-set insecurities I had about my looks.

Spoiler alert: it wasn't.

My flight was booked for the day after the lads' mag *FHM*'s annual awards do – 100 Sexiest Women – which seems so old-fashioned and outdated now but at the time they were huge news and attracted the biggest names in showbiz to attend. That year they'd given me Sexiest British woman which kicked off the usual shower of horrible tweets.

'She's really ugly, why did she get it? She's not even pretty!' All of which, in my head, confirmed I was doing the right thing as I flew to Greece for the nose job with my friend Sarah by my side for moral support. I hadn't told anyone besides Scott and a couple of my closest mates what I was doing, not even my mum, who would have tried to talk me out of it and told me not to mess with my face.

The rhinoplasty was a three-hour surgery and everything went well, but when I came round from the anaesthetic I had a message to tell me Scott was in intensive care.

He'd collapsed in training and after being taken to hospital, they'd discovered a blood clot on his shoulder – he was in a really bad way.

Obviously, I needed to get home. But I was two thousand miles away with my face so swollen and bruised that I looked like something out of a horror movie. I told the surgeon I had to get back to England as quickly as possible, explaining that my boyfriend was in intensive care, but I was warned it was too dangerous to get on a flight so soon after surgery.

The surgeon said I needed to wait a few days, so when I managed to speak to Scott on the phone, I promised him I would be home as soon as I could. Scott was incensed and refused to accept that I couldn't physically get there. After the call, he sent me a long message telling me that we were over.

He said the time apart and being in hospital had given him a chance to reflect on the relationship, and he was disgusted that I'd not moved heaven and earth to get to his bedside.

'I can't believe you've not got here,' he wrote. 'If it was the other way round, I would have got on a boat to come and see you.'

I didn't think it was possible to feel pain like that. Despite our ups and downs, I loved Scott and splitting up was the last thing in the world I wanted and I knew that regardless of what the surgeon said, come hell or high water I needed to get on a flight to try and save the relationship.

I removed my cast and called a taxi to the airport, paying about two grand to get home, flying via Germany to do it as quickly as possible. When I landed in Manchester, I went straight to the hospital.

Scott was sitting up in bed as the nurse showed me into his room.

'Babe,' I said, 'I'm sorry I couldn't get here before now. I love you.'

But he was having none of it. He was so cold with me and would only say he'd made up his mind and didn't want to be together anymore.

I was crying my heart out, so upset that the nurses had to come in to calm me down and I had no choice but to walk away.

I went back to the house we shared in Prestbury only to find his parents there which was, understandably, mega awkward so instead I drove to my parents'.

I was heartbroken. Scott really was my everything.

In my distress, I ended up having a row with my mum,

a horrible shouting match where we both said things we later regretted.

'We need to sort you out, Helen!' she said. 'You're not well.'

I'll give my mum her dues. This time she was dead right.

Chapter Seven

Intrusions

I WAS BARELY HOLDING IT together, but my heartbreak over Scott was actually just the warm-up act. While the next two years would bring times of great happiness and glimmers of hope I clung to as lifelines, there would also be a series of crises to contend with. Including the return of my OCD with such vengeance that I would find myself at the doors of The Priory clinic having run out of ways to pretend I was fine.

When Scott came out of hospital in the second half of May, he was in a better frame of mind and agreed to talk things through. He admitted that I'd borne the brunt of his upset about the horrible news that he needed surgery to remove a rib which would rule him out of football for the next three months. Having had time to think, he now wasn't so sure that he wanted us to finish after all which was music to my ears.

I told him I would do anything to make it work and I meant it.

I didn't want to lose him, and had been thoroughly miserable in the fortnight we'd been apart.

After several conversations, we tentatively agreed to give things another go, but I should have known it was never going to be plain sailing...

In the second week of June 2013, I was booked to go to Ibiza to do a cover shoot with *FHM* magazine which went really well, but in between shots I'd been papped topless on the beach which was gutting. It's a hazard of the job, but a nasty one all the same and it creeped me out to think there had been some man secretly snapping me while I was half-naked.

I soon had far bigger things to worry about when my agent, who was travelling with me, took a call which looked serious and then asked me to sit down.

Oh, fuck. This didn't sound good.

'Helen,' she said, 'I'm sorry to have to tell you this but there's a story coming out in the papers and it looks like Scott's cheated on you.'

It was like my heart stopped. What?!

This couldn't be true, please don't let this be happening. Scott wasn't like other footballers, this wasn't his style. At the time he was on holiday with his family in Dubai, so once I'd steadied myself, I rang him and confronted him with what I'd been told down the telephone line.

He instantly denied everything and I wanted to believe

him so much. I loved him. He said this girl was just desperate to be famous and whatever she was saying, she'd made the whole story up to get her 15 minutes in the spotlight.

I had a horrible, uneasy feeling in the pit of my stomach, and maybe I was kidding myself, but for now at least, I chose to accept his explanation. To this day I don't know for sure what happened, but I was very quick to give Scott the benefit of the doubt. I didn't give him the grilling the story warranted, perhaps because I was subconsciously scared of what would emerge if I pushed too hard.

It's actually embarrassing to remember this because I'm all for female empowerment and if I caught so much as a whiff of any boy cheating on me now, he'd be out on his ear. But I was vulnerable with Scott and I was at such a fragile point, struggling with the ups and downs of my mental health, and under the impression that I depended on him for my survival.

That night I didn't sleep a wink, knowing this story could land any day but not having any specifics beyond the few vague details I'd been told by my agent.

So, this shitshow was bubbling away and it formed the backdrop to what happened next, something which has haunted me ever since. My photographer friend Stacey came up from Wales to stay, and keep me company while Scott was away – satisfied that he'd convinced me there was nothing in this story, he'd chosen not to come home and face the music which I think now is very telling about how important our relationship was (or wasn't) to him at that time.

Me and Stacey had a little sideline business which involved us driving to random locations, doing a super fun lingerie shoot and then selling the photos to the lads' mags like *Nuts* and *Zoo* who would pay thousands to publish them exclusively.

I mean, those were the days!

We were bloody good at what we did, and had such a laugh doing it. On Monday June 17th, we'd done one of those sexy shoots somewhere before coming back to my place for a girls' night in. It was a warm summer's evening and I'd opened the back door in the kitchen to let some cooler air in as I cracked open a bottle of wine while Stacey was upstairs getting changed.

All of a sudden, three men in balaclavas burst into the kitchen through the open back door, shouting at me to do exactly what they said. One of them picked me up, pinned me against the wall and pressed a screwdriver into my face.

'Don't make a sound or I'll skin your fucking face off!' he yelled.

I was terrified. Stacey was at the top of the stairs and she tried to make a run for the front door, but one of the men pulled her back by her hair and I thought we were done for. So many thoughts were racing through my head. I told them they could take whatever they wanted as long as they please, *please* didn't hurt us.

The men took us both upstairs and threw us down on the bed, demanding to know where the safe was. I didn't even know we had a safe! I told them Scott wasn't home and I didn't have a clue where anything was. All I could offer them was a diamond ring he'd given me for my 20th birthday which was worth a few grand and the Rolex he'd given me for my 21st. I said my Audi R8 was on the drive, but warned them that it had a tracker on it – I was trying to be helpful because when you're frightened for your life, honesty feels like the safest policy.

Stacey was thinking of her two young kids back home and had become absolutely hysterical, begging them to let us go and screaming for help, but it's not like anyone outside would have heard us outside. The house was detached, set back from the street by a sweeping driveway and so vast that we could have held a rock concert in the living room and no one would have registered.

One of the guys took me aside into the en suite and said, 'Helen, honestly, we're not going to hurt you. It's going to be OK.'

But rather than being reassured, I found that highly sinister, because who the hell was this guy? Did he know me? Why was he using my name? After that, they took us back downstairs and locked us in the utility room while they ransacked the place. Me and Stacey huddled together on the floor and just held on to each other, shaking and crying.

I'd got it into my head that the men were going to set the

house on fire before they left, and we would be trapped in this room like sitting ducks. But we didn't dare try and escape because the thought of how they might react if the robbers caught us was too awful to contemplate.

My instinct was torn in two. Stay put and risk being burned alive? Or make a run for it and risk ending up in the hands of men who had already shown they could be violent?

I'm not sure how long we stayed in the utility, but when we hadn't heard any movement for a while, I made the decision that we should try and get away.

Despite my jelly legs, I somehow managed to clamber out the window, Stacey followed behind, and the panic and the fear were like nothing else as, powered by adrenaline, we ran like hell for the front gate, not knowing if the men were still there, possibly now in pursuit.

We got out of the gate and legged it first to the house opposite, in the chaos I'd forgotten it was empty, so then we went to the one next door, pressing the buzzer, screaming for someone to come and help us.

The neighbours didn't know what was going on and they answered like, 'What the hell?!' as my legs buckled and I fell to the ground. They brought us inside and before I knew it, there were police everywhere and me and Stacey were being given cups of tea while we recounted what had happened, still in a state of shock. Both of us were traumatised, but so very lucky that we were otherwise unharmed.

I crashed on our landlord's sofa that night. He and his wife were kind enough to take me in, understanding that I couldn't go back to the house. The police were good too, and they had the CCTV footage which clearly showed the three men breaking in although sadly, as far as I'm aware, they were never caught.

In the carnage of that night, I'd almost forgotten the whole cheating story which was still threatening to break any day. That little treat was waiting for me at the weekend just to round everything off.

As weeks go, I've had better.

* * *

It was *the Sun* who eventually ran the exclusive interview with the girl claiming Scott had been sexting her since they'd met on a yacht in St Tropez a few weeks earlier. She said they hadn't slept together, but the paper printed a few of the alleged messages between them and they made me look like a fool. She also claimed he'd told her some bullshit about how 'not to worry about Helen' because we were only 'half and half'.

It didn't take long for the other papers to pick the story up which meant by mid-morning, it was everywhere although Scott was still denying the whole thing to me and saying she was lying. That girl did seem to want to be famous and she went on to do more interviews, milking the situation for all it was worth. It was as if she was enjoying making me suffer. She harassed me on social media, posting sly digs in my direction trying to get a rise out of me, and even wrote an 'open letter' to me in one of the showbiz mags offering me relationship advice for god's sake.

Ignore, ignore, ignore.

Months later, we happened to be on the same flight to LA and as we came out of the airport, she deliberately barged into me before ringing the paper to say we'd had a fight on the plane! So she was engineering her own press and that's a little desperate, right?

Scott had flown back from Dubai in time for the story to drop, having cut short his holiday in the aftermath of the robbery, but instead of putting his arms around me, he was more angry that his watches had been stolen. He wasn't sympathetic at all, he wasn't there for me and almost seemed to blame me for the whole thing.

We were supposed to be going on holiday to Italy, but he cancelled it saying he didn't want to go away with me.

I begged him not to split up with me again. Would I beg a man for anything now? Would I bollocks. I simply wouldn't take that level of crap from anyone these days, but I was so lost when I was younger.

Shellshocked by what had been a harrowing week, I went to stay with my agent in Brighton to get away from it all. I loved Vivian, she was always very kind to me and such funny company, quite eccentric and called everyone 'daaarling'. I adored her and her family, too.

Vivian recognised that I needed some focus and

structure back in my life to take my mind off the personal drama and she booked me loads of jobs which kept me occupied and meant I had good money coming in again. She also signed me up to a new Channel 5 reality show called *Celebrity Super Spa* which saw a group of celebs working in a real-life spa in Liverpool and each partnering up with an apprentice.

It would turn out to be exactly the pick-me-up I needed after a horrible past couple of months, a distraction from the rubbish that was going on privately and – bonus – it also meant I had somewhere to live for four weeks because the production company put us all up in a hotel.

I became firm friends with James 'Arg' Argent from *The Only Way is Essex* and we would spend all our time together. I know the producers were hoping for a show romance to develop and they'd try to push me towards him, dropping hints like, 'Ah, you and Arg are so cute together…' But I was too mixed up over Scott and I didn't even know if I actually fancied Arg although I did like him a lot. He definitely wasn't my usual type. I usually went for sporty guys who were into their health and fitness whereas Arg would eat four Greggs sausage rolls for breakfast.

I think he was probably more into me than I was him, but there was a brief moment of heat between us which felt… weird. We were in my hotel room, lying on the bed while he was stroking my back – I think it *could* have spilled over then, but there was something holding me back. And when that moment passed, it was like it was done. I wasn't over Scott so it would have been a mistake to use Arg as a rebound.

Unfortunately, I didn't get on with everyone quite as well. The TV presenter Yvette Fielding absolutely detested me, and made no secret of it. She even called me 'evil' at one point and gave an interview afterwards saying she didn't know how she'd refrained from slapping me.

Chill out, Yvette! I wasn't *that* bad.

Maybe she wasn't in a great place herself, and I've since read that she went through a very difficult menopause, so I'm going to bear that in mind and try to be kind to her here. I also think she might have forgotten that although we were on a 'reality' TV show, there would be plenty of manipulation by the programme makers in order to create the storylines and build tension.

For instance, on the first day in the salon, the producers wouldn't allow me to go on set for ages. I was keen to get going but they held me back. By the time they eventually let me go on, I was 'late' and I quickly realised they'd kept me on purpose to piss the others off.

Anyway, I came trotting in wearing this little pink uniform and my Louboutins and Yvette took an instant dislike to me.

'Oh, I don't know who you think you are, swanning in here late.'

Like, fully disgusted at me.

'I'm sorry… I'm not sure why you're having a pop at me,' I replied.

From then on she was frostier than the Arctic. I think she thought I was on drugs because one time off-camera, she said, 'You're going to be dead by the time you're 28, you know that?'

What on *earth*?! Who even says that to someone? And I'd seen what drugs can do to people who were close to me and there was no way I'd ever go down that route.

There was a night after filming that I went to an *FHM* party in London – it was all signed off by production who had arranged for a driver to take me there and back. I wore this cool Agent Provocateur dress and had a really good night with my friend, but when I arrived on set the next morning (and this was on camera) Yvette sneered, 'I saw what you wore last night. Wasn't very classy, was it?'

Er, no offence but Yvette Fielding was the last person I'd be taking fashion advice from. She said all this while wearing these terrible shoes, like proper granny clod-hoppers, and although I'm not the sort to disrespect my elders, she was bang out of order.

'Well, I don't think your shoes are very classy either, Yvette,' I replied.

Maybe the producers had asked her to go for me so she was doing a job for them, but she was exactly the same off camera to me as she was on.

Such an odd character.

After the show wrapped, I still had nowhere permanent to live so I rented an apartment at the Hilton in Manchester. I made the place my own a little bit with my Barbie pillowcase, but I can't say I was living my best life there.

There was nothing in the fridge except alcohol and I'd chain smoke all day, putting the cigarettes out in a mug of water which is disgusting and I feel ill to think of the way I was existing.

I'd eat in the morning, have nothing else for the rest of the day and then drink most nights.

Me and Scott were still in touch and he came over to the apartment one day after training – one thing led to another and he ended up staying the night which I thought meant we were getting back together. I assumed that's what he wanted – he'd certainly implied that by his actions.

But the following morning, Scott made it clear he had no intention of taking me back and to rub salt in the wound, he accused me of never putting him first when we'd been together. He'd obviously just wanted to have sex with me which made me feel used and stupid.

I tried to move on. By now it was October and I booked a holiday on my own to the Maldives which was out of my comfort zone, but travelling solo was something I really wanted to do and I did manage to find some peace there.

When I got back, I was booked to do a BBC Three comedy panel show called *Sweat the Small Stuff* which was presented by Nick Grimshaw and had Rochelle Humes and Melvin Odoom as the team captains. The episode I was on also happened to feature James Arthur who had won *The X Factor* in 2012 and you could say that we, erm, hit it off.

Egged on by Grimmy, me and James flirted pretty outrageously throughout the filming and swapped numbers afterwards with a loose arrangement to meet up for a drink in the not too distant future. Nothing ever came of it apart from the exchange of some harmless WhatsApps, but once the episode aired a few days later, the press got hold of it and ran multiple stories saying we were dating.

Scott was livid about it and tried everything he could to get hold of me, ringing my mobile and calling my parents' landline. I didn't want to speak to him. He'd been so horrible to me and I was trying to get over him, something I felt like I was making good progress with.

The thing was though, I still loved him. I dug my heels in for as long as I could, but in the end I was helpless to how I really felt and agreed to meet up.

The Scott I found was a different person to the one who had been so callous to me months before. He apologised for everything as I told him how he used to make me feel and how unkind he could be.

'You're so nasty, Scott. You've got this really mean streak and sometimes I think I'm so much better off without you.'

He promised me that he'd change and stop behaving

like such a dickhead and because I loved him, we got back together. And he really did change. For a while, at least. It felt like we were starting again with a clean slate.

By the end of 2013, we were officially back together and planning our future.

* * *

By this time, Scott was on a season-long loan at West Bromwich Albion, so I moved into his place in Birmingham which was probably my favourite house we ever lived in together. It was so cool and it had a swimming pool which was amazing to me.

We were very happy in those days. It was like a honeymoon period, and Scott was much more attentive with me. I put everything into the relationship because I wanted it to work out for us, he was my first and only love and he knew me inside out.

There's something so special and unique about having a connection like that with one person and sharing all the little in-jokes which only the two of you know about and understand. We used to sign off our WhatsApps to each other TFE which stood for Together Forever, that was our thing.

I know Scott struggled to find his way with his football career and he was frustrated that things weren't going well at Man City, a club he'd joined with such high hopes. And I think he took those tensions out on me simply because I was there. Scott's not a bad person. His behaviour towards me over the years hasn't always been great, but we really did – and still do – love each other.

TFE. Certainly at that time I thought we would be.

Life was good. I had lots of modelling work coming in and was earning decent money. After six months of being blissfully back together and basking in this new, more mature, strong and settled phase of our relationship, we decided we were going to try for a baby.

OK, OK. I know that might sound a bit impulsive given everything I've just documented here and with the benefit of hindsight I can see that myself, but to us it felt like the next logical step. Plus, I'd always wanted to be a young mum. I think I was born broody.

We didn't have to try for very long. It was September 2014, and we were driving down to London to have dinner with some friends – Scott had promised to buy me a Chanel bag while we were there which was probably why I was so keen to go!

However, the promise of a new handbag wasn't the only thing on my mind. I'd missed my period which wasn't like me as I was usually as regular as clockwork, so I knew something was up. As soon as we got checked into our hotel, I nipped to the nearest Boots and bought a pregnancy test.

My heart was beating out of my chest as I waited for the result to appear on the digital screen and when the words appeared, confirming what I already knew deep down, I felt the greatest rush of joy.

I told Scott that it was positive and his jaw dropped to the floor before he broke out into the biggest grin and took me in his arms, both of us elated.

Over the next few months, this baby saved me. Having something beautiful to focus on lifted me out of the fog, the pressures of being in the public eye, the bad times that me and Scott had been through, the traumatic memories of the robbery... Now I had something precious to look forward to, something so innocent. I felt like it was the start of a new chapter, and I was certain that motherhood would be the making of me.

I carried on as if I was the first pregnant woman in the world. Right from the start, it was like, 'I am PREGNANT!' I wanted to shout it from the rooftops, I was delighted and so proud of my growing baby bump.

That said, for the first few months I was really poorly and throwing up multiple times a day. The sickness got progressively worse forcing me to spend most of my time at my parents' house where my mum could look after me while Scott was training.

I was diagnosed with hyperemesis gravidarum (HG), the same condition which Kate Middleton battled throughout each of her three pregnancies and it was horrific.

Believe me when I say this thing is not 'morning sickness'. If only. For me, it got more severe with each pregnancy and by my third I would be hospitalised.

By January 2015, the HG had subsided and I had

entered a new, much more glowing phase of pregnancy. Scott, who had been back at Man City since the start of the season, signed on loan for Aston Villa, and because it had happened quite quickly and we had nowhere organised to live, the club put us up in a hotel.

This meant I spent the rest of my pregnancy living in a suite at the Belfry with room service, unlimited treatments and pregnancy massage on tap which, I'm sure you can imagine, was total and utter hell. Can you think of anything worse? Ha!

I took being 'with child' very seriously. There wasn't really a lot else I could do as this was before social media could be monetised in the way it is now, but I loved the whole nesting period and getting ready to become a mum. We'd decided not to find out the sex and to keep it a surprise although both of us thought it was a boy from day one.

I was nervous as anything about giving birth having heard some horror stories from other women, but I also couldn't wait to meet my baby, and when my contractions started 11 days overdue, I was more than ready.

By the time we got to Goodhope Hospital in Sutton Coldfield, I was four centimetres dilated and well on my way. I was given a private room, but then for some reason, my contractions seemed to stop and we were in overnight with no progress. My pampered Premiership prince Scott had to sleep on a chair which he pronounced in the morning as being 'the worst night' of his life even though I was the one about to push a human out of my vagina.

By then I'd become quite anxious, worried about the baby and why everything had ground to a halt, and yet this was the moment Scott decided he needed to go back home to catch up on some valuable sleep. He left me on my own, something I don't think he should have done, but I suppose we were both young, and maybe he didn't realise what was appropriate behaviour when your partner is in labour.

That's me being generous, by the way…

He returned later that day, just before they broke my waters, and he'd brought with him a Nando's which he tucked into while stinking the room out. Then he FaceTimed his brother so they could sit and watch the boxing together… the midwife just stared at him in disbelief clearly thinking, 'Who even is this idiot?'

At that moment in time, I wasn't even sure myself.

Meanwhile, this baby wasn't budging. I was in such discomfort and it had gone on for so long that I had pethidine, then an epidural. In the end they gave me an episiotomy and used the forceps and finally it was over.

Or just beginning, depending on which way you look at it!

When they announced we had a healthy baby girl, I was floored. It had never entered my head that it might be a girl; I was so convinced the whole time that I was having a boy.

It didn't matter though. The only thing I cared about now was holding my baby in my arms and I was obsessed with her from the second she was born. Both Scott and I were on cloud nine with our 7lbs 6oz beautiful princess daughter, Matilda Jessica Sinclair.

I felt like I was in a dream and couldn't stop staring at her. I thought I must be the luckiest girl in the world, but it was also overwhelming and terrifying. Neither me nor Scott had any idea how to even change a nappy. These days I could change 50 nappies in my sleep and with one hand tied behind my back, but back then we were clueless novices and had to learn on the job.

That was especially true for me as I struggled to get to grips with breastfeeding which was a really important thing for me to do for my baby. My mum had breastfed all four of us, and I was determined to push through the initial pain to do the same for Matilda, slathering on the lanolin to save my poor, cracked nipples.

Mum was a huge support to me in those early weeks and came to stay with me in our new house while Scott was occupied with pre-season training for Villa.

I threw myself headfirst into motherhood, I was consumed by it and savoured every second. I also loved how it brought me and my mum closer after our relationship had taken such a battering over the last few years.

I found joy in the simple things. Pushing the pram around Bolton town centre, walks in the park, popping to the supermarket with Matilda in the baby carrier.

Mundane, everyday ordinariness, which I'd normally have found quite boring now felt dreamy because I was doing it with my gorgeous baby girl.

I liked the fact I was suddenly under the radar and no longer in the press day to day. For so many years a lot of things in my life had been destructive and complicated and now I had something to focus on which was healing and pure.

The future felt so hopeful. Scott had built a beautiful family home in the Surrey village of Oxshott with stunning marble floors, a vast staircase and a swimming pool, and the plan was for us to live there when he retired. As a family, we were set for life thanks to football and his shrewd investments, although there was always a nagging thought in my head that I didn't own anything myself.

None of Scott's properties were in my name and we weren't married, so I had no financial security and I had to just trust that he would do right by me.

Apart from that, there was a lot to look forward to and I was never happier than when I had my little girl in my arms.

But blighting that joy was the return of the intrusive thoughts which had troubled me off and on since childhood and were now threatening to shatter my baby bubble. They kind of crept up on me at first, starting with a bit of fretting over whether Matilda had taken enough milk – was her tummy full enough, had I fed her properly? – but would then spiral into completely irrational scenarios in my head that she was going to die because I'd starved her.

What if she died? It would be my fault. What if I died? What would happen to her?

I started to obsess about germs and didn't want other people touching Matilda in case they passed something on. I didn't trust anyone else with my baby, sometimes not even Scott. I remember once being in the shower while a very good friend of mine was downstairs watching Matilda. I got it into my head that this person was physically hurting my baby – I was up here in the bathroom, not able to do anything about it and Matilda would never be able to tell me. It was a level of panic and paranoia I'd never felt before and I just lost all confidence in my abilities as a mother.

I didn't even like burping her because I thought it would hurt her. My thoughts would constantly tell me I had harmed my baby and, of course, I hadn't – I loved her to pieces and would never have hurt a hair on her head. But I'd get so distressed by these intrusive thoughts that they'd cause a panic attack. When you're in the midst of an OCD episode like this, you can't think with any clarity or rationale.

Every time I went upstairs, I'd think I was going to chuck her over the top of the bannister, and I saw those images flash through my mind as clear as day of me letting go and watching Matilda fall.

I can't go near those stairs because if I do, I'm going to throw her. I'll hold her over the top and let her go. I'm a dreadful, evil mother.

My mind became a battlefield; these thoughts would arrive like uninvited guests and then refuse to leave. They were vivid and often violent. It was brutal and relentless.

Each thought felt like confirmation of something monstrous within me. Who even was I? What sort of sick and twisted person must I be? I didn't feel disconnected from Matilda, not ever, but I was completely terrified of myself.

I loved her so much I ached and that's what made the thoughts all the more unbearable.

But I couldn't tell anyone, because they'd think I was a terrible human being and maybe my baby would be taken away from me.

There was no peace, not even in sleep because I started to experience anxiety nightmares. Matilda slept in a Moses basket next to the bed, but I'd wake up screaming and barely able to breathe, thinking she was stuck in our duvet and suffocating.

It would take me a long time to calm down and I don't think Scott knew how to handle it. He'd get exasperated with me and couldn't understand where all this angst was coming from.

At my lowest points I thought about taking my own life. I didn't want to be here and thought everyone might be better off without me. Matilda deserved someone better than me.

I want to emphasise here that I truly loved being a mum, but when the anxiety and the OCD barged their way in and took control of my head, I was defenceless.

It's such a frightening illness because the thoughts are so lucid that they completely warp your reality, convincing you that things have happened which haven't.

A few months after I had Matilda, my friends persuaded me to come along on a night out in Birmingham – I wasn't in the right frame of mind for it and I should never have gone. Across the nightclub I noticed a guy who had red lipstick marks all over his face and in my head I thought, 'Oh my God, I've just shagged him in the toilet! I can't believe I've just cheated on Scott!'

My friends were telling me that this was impossible because I'd been with them the whole time, but I became so overwrought that I had to be taken home.

The thoughts were so suffocating it felt like they might kill me and I booked an appointment with the doctor who suggested I was suffering from postnatal depression and offered to prescribe antidepressants. I refused any medication. I didn't want to be on anything, I'd stopped taking Concerta during the pregnancy and while I was breastfeeding and this had felt like a positive change.

Back then I had no idea there was a name for what I was experiencing, I just thought I was cracking up and off my head. It wouldn't be until I got hold of Bryony Gordon's brilliant book *Mad Girl* in the summer of 2016 that everything started to make sense. She talked so candidly about her OCD – which was something I'd previously thought was to do with people who like their houses clean and tidy, or David Beckham lining up his cans of Pepsi neatly in the fridge.

I'd never linked the condition to intrusive thoughts, but everything Bryony was describing, I recognised in myself and I realised there was a reason behind all this.

I wasn't a weirdo.

My brain was just wired in a different way, and if someone had told me that years ago, it might have saved me a lot of grief and self-loathing. And that's why I'm talking about this now and being open about the horrific thoughts I was plagued by because if there's anyone reading this going through something similar and it makes them feel less alone, then I'm doing a good thing.

By March 2016 when Matilda was nine months old, it was really bad. Out of control.

My social anxiety was through the roof. I didn't feel I could see anyone and that made life quite lonely. It was such a shame because the wives and girlfriends at Aston Villa were lovely and they always made me feel so welcome, but I couldn't do it.

The only people I was able to be around were Scott, my mum and my gay best friend, Jay. I'd go to watch Scott play at the weekend, but I'd get worked up for hours before, hoping that no one would speak to me.

Please God, don't let anyone notice me. Don't let them try and talk to me.

And the saddest thing is, there were definitely girls there I could have been friends with, but I didn't have it in me. My hands would get shaky and then I'd feel embarrassed, thinking people were going to realise that I was in a state. That would play in my head and any conversation I had, however brief, would torment me for days afterwards as I analysed it over and over. If I could have hidden away and never had to interact with another human being, I totally would have.

The anxiety was causing the pounds to drop off me and I became very thin.

I couldn't escape the thoughts.

We'd started weaning Matilda on to solids, but I could never feed her until Scott came home from training because I was too scared she would choke.

Scott was mostly oblivious to how bad things were. Or at least he pretended to be. He tends not to notice much other than football; he's not in touch with his emotions and has never been clued up on mental health, so he was at a loss.

It all came to a head when my mum took me to The Priory as an outpatient and I started attending therapy sessions weekly for the next year. The therapist explained to me that the thoughts didn't make me a bad person and my baby wasn't going to be taken away. She told me that intrusive thoughts were not uncommon and could be especially heightened after childbirth.

I told her this was something I'd been fighting since I was a young girl and as soon as I talked about it, I started to feel a little bit better, like a vice which had been clamped around my head slowly being released. Through therapy, I learned that the thoughts weren't dangerous and that I wasn't dangerous either. The fact I was horrified by them was the biggest indicator I would never act on them.

I had to learn to accept my thoughts were not me.

But that OCD is an evil little fucker.

And even though I was starting to find a way through the fog this time, it wasn't done with me. Not by a long way.

Chapter Eight

New Beginnings

OF ALL THE PLACES I'VE lived, I don't think I've ever been as settled as when I was lucky enough to call Glasgow my home. By the start of the 2016/17 season, Scott had signed a four-year deal with Celtic and we were moving north of the border as a family of three to begin our Scottish adventure.

For the first two months we were based in the seriously swanky Blythswood Square Hotel and Spa, which was fantastic but, admittedly, not ideal with a young child. We needed a family home with space for all Matilda's stuff (she had a better and more extensive wardrobe than me!) and a garden for her to play in, and we found the perfect place in the West End.

If you don't know it, Glasgow's West End is a really cool, vibrant area of the city and the whole move felt like a much-needed fresh start for all of us.

It was transformative in every way. Scott was enjoying his football again – he scored the winner on his debut against Hearts and put himself in the club's history books by finding the back of the net in each of his first five matches. The fans instantly took him to their hearts; he was loved by them and whenever they sang his name I just about burst with pride.

> *'Oh, he's Scotty Sinclair and he is so wonderful,*
> *When he scores a goal oh, it's beautiful, magical,*
> *When he runs down the wing he is fast as lightning, it's frightening and it makes all the bhoys sing...'*

After years of struggling to make his mark on the game, he'd found a club where he slotted straight in.

Glasgow itself had all the life and soul of Manchester, but none of the press attention or memories of past mistakes, and it was so peaceful just to be left to live our lives as a normal family.

I found a lovely group of female friends who had children of similar ages, especially Sarah Hayes, who was married to Celtic player Jonny Hayes – she was one of those mega-organised mums who always had snacks and activities handy. Her house was immaculate too, and I'd always wonder, how does this woman do it?

There was also Libby, a single mum with a little boy born a week apart from Matilda – I loved being around her, she was such a positive spirit and she made me double over laughing. We used to go to baby classes together, but would only ever make the last ten minutes because I was always so late picking her up.

I was through the worst of the OCD at this point and Libby put me in touch with an amazing woman called Miriam to help me with my social anxiety, a lady I still see now. She's not a therapist, she's more of an energy healer and she's an incredibly special person. Miriam helped me form a different, more positive mindset and thanks to her and my regular therapy sessions, I felt stronger and more in control of my mental health.

The intrusive thoughts were still there from time to time, but I understood them so much better now and began to consider whether I might be well enough to return to work in some way. I loved being a mummy, but after more than four years out of acting, I had an itch. I wanted to do *something*.

But I was also worried about slipping back again having come so far in the last six months. I remembered only too well how fragile I'd been when I'd made the decision to quit *Corrie* back in 2012.

However, the stars seemed to be aligning because around the same time I was mulling all this over, I caught up with Brooke Vincent and the conversation turned to what it would be like if I was to come back to *Corrie*.

What would Rosie be up to? How would she fit into life on the street? Who would she be dating? What trouble would she be causing? We had a giggle over the potential storylines for Rosie and Sophie who, despite being sisters, were such different characters.

I'm not too sure of the exact chain of events that followed, but as far as I know, Brooke mentioned our chat to the producer, that I'd be open to a comeback and I was contacted shortly afterwards about the possibility of a return.

OK, now I had a decision to make. A big one.

Scott didn't want me to go back. He didn't understand why I'd even contemplate it and told me I didn't need to do it. We had a lovely life in Scotland, everything was going great and if it ain't broke, why fix it?

I totally got that. But, in a way, I *did* need to. I needed to do it for me.

It was going to mean a weekly train commute between Glasgow and Manchester with an 18-month-old in tow, not a task for the faint-hearted. But my mum said she'd do everything she could to help us, volunteering to look after Matilda whenever I was at work so we wouldn't need to worry about finding a nanny. Matilda was her first grandchild and she was desperate to spend time with her. She missed us so much since we'd moved to Scotland.

Maybe I was crazy. Maybe this was the most ridiculous move I'd ever make (and I've made a few), but in February 2017, I boarded a train at Glasgow Central and made my way down to Manchester to film my first scenes back as Rosie Webster.

At first I loved being back. I became really good friends with Lucy Fallon, who played Bethany Platt, and it was wonderful spending my days with Brooke who always brings such good energy. I love the bones of that girl.

But at the same time, a lot had changed and the place felt quite different to the one I'd left behind five years before. There were cliques amongst the cast which seemed a bit exclusionary, and I was made to feel particularly uncomfortable by another actress who could be quite sarcastic and cold with me.

Maybe her nose was out of joint because my return had attracted a fair bit of press attention – not something I could have helped – but I do think she had a false impression of me. She'd once asked me something in the green room and got the wrong end of the stick because I was on the phone and so it looked like I'd ignored her. Perhaps she thought I was stuck up.

The thing is, she was quite popular with the rest of the cast – a bit of a leader of the pack – and because she was unpleasant to me and had made it clear I wasn't welcome, I'd end up sitting on my own a lot of the time in the canteen feeling quite left out.

It was like a real-life *Mean Girls* when I think about it now.

I can get on with everyone, but this actress just wasn't very nice to me. I didn't make a fuss about it, I just wanted to get on with the job.

Suck it up, Helen.

But it wasn't long before I started to feel a bit frustrated with what I thought were the lack of storylines for Rosie. I'd been used to being one of the central characters and I'd been key to two spin-off series in the past, but now Rosie was a bit of an incidental and was only being written comedically. Don't get me wrong, I really enjoyed the entertaining side of her and valued the creative input I was given. For instance, when I saw the writers had made Rosie a window cleaner, which was the least Rosie thing *ever*. I went to see the producer and said if we were going to do this, she would have to be in pink sparkly overalls and a matching fluffy handbag. At least keep it in character.

But I missed being part of the bigger stories where I could be pushed and challenged as an actress. I didn't want to be coming all the way down from Scotland, carting Matilda with me, just to say a few lines.

Adding insult to injury was the meeting I had after a few months to negotiate a contract extension as well as my salary, where I was informed that there would be no pay rise because I wasn't a 'leading lady.' That cut.

Although, to be honest, I had a load of other things on my mind. Well, one thing, really. My period was late.

* * *

At first I thought I must have got my dates mixed up. There had been one night a few weeks before where me and Scott had got carried away and hadn't been too careful, but I'd told myself it would be fine.

I didn't want another baby at that time. I wanted to focus on my career for a while.

When I couldn't put it off any longer, I did a pregnancy test at my mum's while Scott was in Dubai (where else?) and lo and behold, it came up positive. I didn't know what to think or feel, only that I knew this wasn't part of my plan.

Now of course, I love Delilah to absolute death – thank God for Delilah! – but at the time I was knocked for six. At 27, I felt too young to have two children and there were still periods where things between me and Scott weren't right; it didn't feel like a very stable environment to be bringing a baby into.

I was often unsure about what the future of our relationship looked like.

We'd actually split up for about two weeks when I first started again at *Corrie* and although we loved each other, and the passion was still there, sometimes it was as if we were worlds apart and small misunderstandings could very easily descend into full-blown rows.

I was properly nervous about sharing the news with Scott and didn't know how he was going to react. I waited till he got home to tell him and to my surprise, he was ecstatic! I've got a photo of him holding the pregnancy test with this huge smile on his face and it's still my favourite ever picture of him.

He was delighted about the prospect of becoming a dad again, but I also think he was secretly pleased that maternity leave would mean I wouldn't be travelling back and forth to Manchester anymore, and we could be together more often as a family. And I was lifted by seeing how happy he was; my doubts ebbed away and I started to think that this baby could be the perfect addition.

That happiness was short-lived though, because just as with Matilda, I started to get extremely poorly. This time round the hyperemesis gravidarum was even more vicious, especially because I was working full-time at *Corrie* and having to commute while battling this violent sickness, unable to keep anything down.

I'd throw up outside the station, in the station, on the train… it was beyond grim and getting worse with every week.

Scott and I had moved out of the West End flat and into a beautiful high-ceilinged apartment in Bearsden, a leafy town to the north of Glasgow and I had a lovely lady called Pauline, who would come and help me with Matilda and the house once a week whenever I wasn't in Manchester.

There was one day I was laid up on the sofa and in quite a lot of pain and Pauline said, 'I can't leave you like this… I think you need to go to hospital.'

I insisted I was fine, but when Scott came home, he could see how my condition had deteriorated and immediately called the Celtic doctor to come over and see me. The doctor was worried that I was having an ectopic pregnancy, and told us we had to get to hospital as quickly as possible.

Thankfully, that turned out to be a false alarm, but the doctors who examined me said the pain I was in was from a water infection from being so severely dehydrated after constantly throwing up for days on end. They put me on a drip and gave me the sickness medication cyclizine. I had never taken any meds when pregnant with Matilda – not even my daily ADHD pills – and I really didn't want to this time either, but I was just so sick at that stage that I didn't have a choice. I was physically and emotionally drained with nothing left in the tank.

While I was in such a bad way, I couldn't work which I know was a massive headache for everyone at *Coronation Street* because schedules are planned very far in advance, and it costs time and money to write you out of ongoing storylines. It was tough for me too, because I'd had the mentality from a young age that you turn up to work unless you've got a limb hanging off.

But any woman who has had hyperemesis gravidarum will know that it's a living hell. It completely incapacitates you and makes everyday functioning pretty much impossible. You can't ease it with a couple of Jacob's crackers and some ginger tea like you can morning sickness.

It's misery on steroids and turns you into a vomiting zombie. I couldn't look after Matilda, I couldn't take her anywhere, I couldn't drive, I wasn't even able to summon up the strength to crawl to the fridge to make my daughter some food.

I'd lost a lot of weight and would cry with sheer exhaustion. My friend used to come round to wash my hair for me because I was bed-bound most of the time and my mum came to stay for a while – between her and Scott, they managed the load with Matilda, but it was so miserable and depressing.

Once the medication started to kick in, it took the edge off the constant sickness, I still had bouts of nausea, but it was nothing like as bad as it had been as the day I'd been forced to go to hospital. And then when I got to about three months, it cleared almost completely, although by then I was tiny from the weight loss.

At least I was able to travel again, so I returned to *Corrie* and worked throughout the rest of my pregnancy, coming very close to my due date with the directors finding novel ways to hide my bump. Large handbags, strategically positioned tables and boxes of files were all used to disguise my tummy as obviously Rosie wasn't pregnant in the show.

I was grateful that my two experiences with HG hadn't progressed much beyond the first trimester because I understood that for some women, including Kate Middleton, it continued right the way through their pregnancy. But it's also a condition which tends to get more severe with each pregnancy, something I'd find out for myself when I had Charlie three years later.

* * *

Now that I was pregnant again, I felt certain Scott was going to propose. My friends were telling me that he needed to get his finger out, and I thought he was probably going to do it over Christmas.

We'd been getting on well since I'd found out we were having a second and we did a gorgeous shoot together for *OK!* at Cameron House on Loch Lomond. Scott never relished doing magazine shoots, he found it all so awkward, but he did them for me because he knew I enjoyed them and that they'd become part of my job.

And also because I made him do it, ha!

I found his willingness to grin and bear it for my sake really sweet because he was quite a private person and I knew this wasn't in his comfort zone at all.

But I'd become fixed on wanting to be engaged to have that solid commitment from him. I'd see a lot of our footballing friends getting married and I used to feel a bit embarrassed that we had a baby together, another one on the way, but no plans to wed.

If I ever brought it up with Scott, however, he'd bat it away.

'I don't understand why we have to get married,' he'd say. 'What's the big deal?'

Well, it was a big deal to me.

For some reason, I'd convinced myself he was going to propose on Christmas Day. I'm not even sure why I was so certain because he'd not dropped any hints, but maybe I thought he'd use the occasion to surprise me.

As we were unwrapping our gifts that morning, it became apparent that I'd got my hopes up for nothing. Scott had bought me loads of presents including a beautiful Dior handbag, which of course I was grateful for, but there was nothing in the shape of a little box and because I'd built it up so much in my head, when it dawned on me that he had no intention of proposing, it ended up in a massive argument.

He told me I was spoiled. I told him he obviously didn't love me enough.

This shouting match was going on while Matilda was sitting in the corner in her little red dress, happy as Larry with all her presents, oblivious to the fact her mum and dad were going at each other hammer and tongs to the point where at one stage the Christmas tree went flying.

We were booked in at the Blythswood for our Christmas dinner and even though neither of us were in the mood to share a meal together, it was either that or we all went hungry. But the atmosphere was tense to say the least.

After that, I decided to drop the engagement chat, as it was only causing upset, and I couldn't be dealing with the stress when I was pregnant. I'd more or less let go of any hope he was ever going to do it, but during football's three-week winter break in January 2018, we went on holiday to Dubai and while we were there Scott casually suggested that we went to the jeweller's Cara to try some rings on.

I didn't ask too many questions for fear of scaring him

off again, but chose one that I loved with an oval-shaped diamond and Scott said to just leave it with him.

So I left it. And left it. And left it some more.

Another five months went by before he actually asked me to marry him – God knows why he waited until I was the size of a whale and about to pop, but there are a lot of things that Scott did (and does) which make my mind boggle.

To be fair, the proposal when it eventually happened, was super cute. We'd travelled to Disneyland Paris for a family break, although my suitcase had been stolen off the Eurostar that morning, and so I'd arrived without even a clean pair of knickers to my name. I wore the same dress for three days in a row because I had nothing else with me.

Scott had hired an area outside the Disney castle and arranged for a photographer to be there and there were fireworks going off as he got down on one knee, me with my swollen ankles, glasses, no make-up and hair scraped up in a messy bun.

After all this time, he'd caught me off guard all right. And obviously I said yes!

It wasn't how I'd ever imagined my engagement to be, but none of it mattered because I was too busy being over the moon that we were finally engaged. I had the ring on my finger and that was a really big thing for me because I was the mother of Scott's children and I thought it was about him showing respect for that.

I wanted to start planning the wedding straightaway, but Scott proved less keen. It was as if he thought he'd done what I wanted by getting engaged and as far as he was concerned, that was the job done. It was a symbolic act to him rather than anything he intended to see through.

Every time I asked him for his input on whether we should do this or that, or look at certain venues, he was never remotely bothered. He wasn't ever horrible about it, but there was this complete lack of interest and I wanted him to be excited about it just like I was.

It had to be put on the backburner for the time being anyway because I was just about ready to drop and Scott distracted me with a new Range Rover wrapped in a huge pink bow which he said was my 'push present'. Within 48 hours of that, I was in labour.

My mum was staying with us at the time and the two of us had gone to Pret a Manger to pick up some breakfast – I also had to pop to the post office up the hill, but suddenly realised that there was no way I could walk there.

'Mum, I've got to go home,' I said. 'I need to go now.'

Although I was able to drive us back to the house, I was in a lot of discomfort which had become actual pain by the time we arrived home. The kind of pain I recognised only too well, having done this once before.

I started bouncing about on my pregnancy ball, but it wasn't long before the contractions were coming every few minutes and I knew we had to get to hospital. My mum couldn't find the car keys to drive me there and I was trying to remain calm and hold my tongue while she scrabbled around like a headless chicken.

Keys located, we got in the car with Matilda as Scott was out at training and bless her, she was in the back saying 'Just breathe, Mummy!'

We got to the maternity ward at the Queen Elizabeth University Hospital in Glasgow around lunchtime, and my mum called Scott to tell him he needed to leave training and come to the hospital. Like, now.

Things were progressing very quickly and by the time Scott arrived, I was seven centimetres dilated and mooing like a cow. I was pleased to see he'd not brought himself a Nando's this time and there was no FaceTiming his brother either. He'd learned his lesson.

My mum took Matilda home and I got into the birthing pool which was great because it really did take the pain away.

And that's where my beautiful little Delilah Ruby Sinclair was born, in the water on June 22nd 2018 after what felt like an explosion. She actually swam up to meet me and the feeling was indescribable.

Delilah was a blonde-haired baby with bright blue eyes which was so unusual given she's mixed-race. Obviously I love all my children equally, but when I was carrying Delilah I always felt there was something a little bit spiritual and special about her.

The whole aftermath was a completely different experience compared to Matilda, and both me and Delilah took to breastfeeding really easily – I had none of the discomfort or self-consciousness I'd experienced when feeding the first time. Back then, I'd been worried about people getting a flash of a nipple whereas now I couldn't have given less of a flying fig if anyone had seen my entire areola.

Baby needs fed? Whack her on the boob!

I had the benefit of experience by then and age, too.

With everything and everyone healthy, we were discharged the next day to start life as a family of four, and I was hoping for a smooth few days of figuring it out and finding our feet. But then Matilda, who was still only seven, did something which threw me. She'd always been a prim and proper little princess, a real girly girl and never a spot of bother, but within 24 hours of me being home, she produced what I can only describe as a detonation of shit all over the lounge.

I'd only left her the living room for a couple of minutes but when I went back in, there was poo *everywhere*. She was playing with it, smearing it all over the floor and walls with her toy kitchen knives and forks.

It was an absolute disaster zone and I let out an involuntary scream. My mum came rushing in and she was like, 'OH MY GOD!'

'I'll get the bleach, get Matilda out of here!' said my mum, taking charge.

Bless Matilda's little heart. She wasn't being naughty, but I did wonder if it was a reaction to the new baby, like a toddler version of a dirty protest! It was so unlike her, but I guess it's easy to forget that having a newborn is a time of extreme upheaval for the children already here. Everything they've ever known has just changed overnight and will never be the same again.

I can reflect and empathise like this now, but my first thought was, 'Oh my fucking god, if this is what's in store for me, how am I ever going to cope with two kids?'

But of course, we coped – you have no choice but to because there isn't a spare second in the day. And Delilah was the cutest little baby. I dressed her head to toe in pink, took her for walks in our traditional Silver Cross pram, and I have very happy memories of that time. I was engaged, Matilda and Delilah were my dream girls, Scott's football career was going from strength to strength and everything seemed quite perfect.

On top of that, my mental health seemed... robust. Knowing this time what to look for, I was watching like a hawk for the signs of the postnatal OCD and was fully prepared for the intrusive thoughts to rear their ugly heads again. I wasn't scared of it, I knew how this thing worked and I had the tools and confidence to deal with it.

But it didn't happen. I was still having therapy which definitely helped and I felt much better equipped to deal with it this time if history had repeated itself.

However, you'll know by now that nothing in my life stays on an even keel for long.

* * *

When Delilah was about three months old, I started getting private messages via my social media saying Scott had cheated on me with some glamour model.

The first one came through in September 2019 while I was at Disney on Ice at Glasgow's Braehead Arena, and the contrast of having my innocent girls there dressed in their princess outfits, while reading these disgusting messages saying Scott had been playing away, was horrific. I was distraught.

Just like the last time, Scott swore blind it wasn't true, but it was extremely upsetting reading those messages and my mind whirred – he'd definitely had the opportunity to cheat when he was overnighting before away games. But then again, some people are just troublemakers and who can you really trust on social media? Did I take the allegations of a perfect stranger, who wouldn't even use their real name or the word of the man I loved and who was the father of my two children?

Whatever the truth and despite Scott's denials, I was in bits. My mind took me to some horrible places where I got myself worked up about the risk of Scott passing on an STI to me. I was a young woman who had just had a baby, so I was especially vulnerable and I started questioning myself, thinking maybe it was my fault and maybe I'd pushed him away. We'd not been having regular sex because I had a newborn and a toddler – I was breastfeeding, co-sleeping with Delilah and permanently knackered and so 'getting it on' was often the last thing on my mind. Scott was sleeping on a mattress on the floor in the spare room.

My gut feeling now, all these years later, is that people were probably just making things up; it had all come from anonymous accounts, no one had the courage to show themselves or tell me to my face. I don't think internet trolls realise or perhaps even care that the people they are targeting are normal human beings trying to live their lives and when we see messages like that, they have a real impact.

I told Scott I believed him and I tried to forget what I'd read, but those messages had definitely planted a seed. How could they not? As much as I fought it, I started to develop some trust issues.

Scott was good at looking after me and the girls in so many ways. He doted on Matilda and Delilah. But I just don't know. I didn't always feel loved enough by him.

Whether he was cheating or not, there was something seriously adrift.

Chapter Nine

Periods of Hell

LET'S GET REAL FOR A minute. Anyone who works on social media, and bangs on about how hard they work, and what a high-pressure job it is, is a twat. Sorry, not sorry, if that offends anyone.

Sure, content creators put the effort in, they have to meet deadlines and deliver for the brands who are paying them, but there's not a lot more to it than that.

Hard work is being a police officer or working in the fire service or being on the frontline of the NHS. I've got mates with 'normal' jobs who are stuck working long, punishing hours for not much reward, and I simply can't deal with well-paid influencers who make out they've got a tough gig.

Influencing or content creation, whatever you want to label it, is a bloody brilliant job! It's often lucrative, you can work from home a lot of the time, and the hours are flexible. What's not to like?

By the time Delilah had come along, I was earning a very good income purely through social media. Over the previous year or so, the influencer industry had really taken off and there was no shortage of brands who wanted to work and collaborate with me, which was a very fortunate position to be in. I actually did a job for the jewellery company, Abbott Lyon, when Delilah was just two days old.

Even though Scott was one of Celtic's top earners and there was no need for me to work, I liked having my own money even if the work wasn't always exactly what I wanted to do – coming from a working class background I understood the value and importance of grafting and bringing in a wage, however you do it.

I remember doing a job once for Papa John's where I had to get dressed up in a jungle outfit and eat BBQ ostrich pizza as part of some competition promotion. It was such good money that I couldn't turn it down, but as I posed for these not-very-glamourous shots, I do remember thinking, 'How did it come to this? I wanted to be shooting for Vogue magazine!'

But I really wasn't too fussed about what the work was and while I always had the intention to go back to acting, I was also running my maternity lingerie brand, Delilah Ruby, which was doing really well.

On top of that, I was picking up bits and bobs of TV work here and there, like *Celebrity Catchphrase* (I'm normally totally pants on these shows but I enjoy doing them and they pay well) and everything was ticking along OK.

Scott and I were getting on, I'd swerved the postnatal depression I'd been steeling myself for and, best of all, I wasn't having periods. Exclusive breastfeeding can put a stop to your menstrual cycle. It's the body's clever way of spacing out pregnancies and trying to make sure you don't conceive while still nursing a newborn, and the reason why this was such a huge relief to me was because my periods had become a problem, which had snowballed as the years had gone on.

I'd got my first one at 15 which was late compared to most other girls; I'd been so desperate to start, but I think my eating disorder had messed up my system and slowed everything down. I had this terrible fear my sister Jessica, who is two years younger than me, was going to start before me.

I went to a girls' school so there was always a lot of period chat and all my friends had started. There was just me and one other girl in my class who were still period-less and when she got hers, I was so embarrassed and wondered what was wrong with me.

I remember exactly when and where it finally happened. I was at the Octagon Theatre in Bolton where we'd been to watch *A Midsummer Night's Dream* and when I went to the toilet and saw blood on my knickers, I could have punched the air with joy! It was only very light, but it was an unmistakable real-life period and I was soooo happy.

How little I knew…

After that first period, I didn't have another one for about a year which made it all a bit of an anti-climax, but they came back (and then some) when I was 16 along with an eruption of acne which, I'm sure you can appreciate, was delightful for me. What a time to be alive!

Almost overnight I was covered in spots which made me feel so ugly and self-conscious – Alison King at *Corrie* would assure me that no one was looking at or thinking about my skin as much as I was, but I still felt rotten. And, lo and behold, the monthly mood swings also now came as part of the package. I wouldn't make the connection until much later on, but every four weeks, around the time of my period, I'd be on the edge, depressed and suffer these dramatic meltdowns.

This physical, mental and emotional response to my cycle has heightened and worsened over the years and it's something that's now been diagnosed as premenstrual dysphoric disorder or PMDD, a severe and chronic form of premenstrual syndrome.

I know exactly when I'm ovulating because I actually *feel* the chemical shift in my brain. That grey cloud moves into place and so begins a fortnight of irritability, manic behaviour and bouts of depression. I start over-analysing and thinking I'm a failure. It makes me so bloated I look pregnant and I become ridiculously critical of myself which then feeds into my OCD, acting as a catalyst for the most disturbing thoughts.

HEAD & HEART

I get anxious and it affects my relationships, my sleep and my energy, draining me of any motivation. And then as soon as I bleed, it's almost like the hormones all balance out and I have peace and stability again. It's this massive relief and I'll be fine for a fortnight until I ovulate and the whole thing starts again.

It's like I have four different personalities across each month.

What is PMDD?

According to the International Association for Premenstrual Disorders (www.iapmd.com), a PMDD diagnosis requires at least five of the following symptoms, including at least one core (*) emotional symptom.

- Emotional symptoms
- Severe mood swings*
- Irritability or anger which is often intense and/or frequent
- Depressed mood or feelings of hopelessness*
- Anxiety or tension*
- Feeling overwhelmed
- Increased sensitivity to rejection or interpersonal conflict*
- Energy and cognitive symptoms
- Fatigue or low energy
- Sleep disruption – either insomnia or excessive sleep
- Loss of interest in usual activities or relationships
- Difficulty concentrating
- Physical symptoms
- Breast tenderness or swelling
- Headaches
- Joint or muscle pain
- Bloating or weight gain
- Cramps
- Changes in appetite

I'll never forget my first period after having Delilah. It was horrific and, I think, unlocked a whole new level of PMDD. It walloped me so hard that I went to see the GP, who prescribed the antidepressant sertraline which, I think, was a kneejerk reaction. Sertraline really didn't agree with me, so I didn't take it for long and it wasn't treating the right condition anyway or getting to the root cause.

I didn't have postnatal depression – I wasn't clinically depressed. This was all linked to my cycle and my ongoing battle with it. I've read recently that PMDD is more common in women with ADHD so I didn't stand much of a chance, did I?

ADHD, OCD, PMDD…all the bloody Ds.

I wouldn't actually get a handle on it until 2024 and it was mainly thanks to my friend, Grace Prosser, who trains women in cycle syncing which is a wellness approach where you adjust your diet, exercise, work and lifestyle to align with the phases of your menstrual cycle. The idea is to work *with* your body's hormonal fluctuations rather than against them and this will improve energy, mood, productivity and overall health.

It's kind of like a therapy for when you're in your luteal phase – the time just before your period starts – and it's about really drilling down and getting to know the four different stages of your cycle. Grace is quite spiritual and also practices womb healing which I know can sound quite woo-woo to some, but I went to see her every month for four months and she honestly changed my life. I love her to pieces for what she's done for me.

Grace has taught me how to feel my emotions rather than fight them and embrace my feminine energy. I cry when I need to cry, get angry when I'm angry and I allow myself to feel sad if that's what my mind and body are experiencing. I also take the Elle Sera Golden Pill, a plant-based supplement which has helped with my energy levels.

At least I'm now armed with the knowledge to help and support my daughters if the same thing happens to them. Too many women sit there suffering in silence because if we dare to speak up, we're dismissed as being 'too hormonal' or (and this is the worst) 'hysterical', but what I was going through every month is not normal. And I'd urge anyone out there who recognises the symptoms I've described to seek medical help and not to take no for an answer. Alongside other PMDD warriors like Vicky Pattison (I love that girl) I'll keep shouting about this and using whatever platform I have to make as much fuss as possible and help other women. Staying silent isn't an option for me.

* * *

In January 2020, Celtic sold Scott to Preston North End, bringing the curtain down on his career in Scotland and our lovely life as a family in Glasgow. We were both bitterly disappointed to be moving, but I think Celtic needed the money they'd save from having him off the wage bill, and Preston had come in with the sort of offer they couldn't refuse.

That's the way the cookie crumbles for footballers and their families. It's a well-rewarded job financially, but it's often unpredictable and the life can be very transient so you have to be prepared to up sticks and move without much notice.

Scott headed down to Preston first and lived in a hotel while I came back and forth with the kids, splitting our time between there and Scotland. We still had the lease on our apartment in Bearsden and the plan was to do that until we found somewhere more permanent to live back in England.

But then Covid struck and the whole world stopped.

I was freaking out watching the news as this story unfolded. It felt earth-shattering. I was terrified of what the future held, terrified of catching the virus, terrified of losing people I loved. And when it became clear a national lockdown was imminent, me and Scott had to make a decision. At the time, no one knew how long this was going to continue and so the four of us had to form a plan to be in one place together.

Scott said he didn't want to isolate at my parents' house. With professional football about to be suspended and all the training grounds and facilities shut down, he needed to keep up his fitness independently. He argued, quite reasonably, that doing that would be impossible at my mum and dad's in the middle of Bolton.

At his family's house in Bath, there's a running track at the back and loads of land so he'd be able to use it to stay fit until playing resumed.

'I need to be there,' he said. 'You can stay at your mum and dad's with the kids if you want, but I have to be in Bath.'

It wasn't really a choice because I accepted that we needed to stay together, wherever it was, so the four of us all moved into the house Scott had bought for his parents a few years before. It's a massive property so there was plenty of room, and also an annexe where Scott's brother Jake, his girlfriend and their little daughter were staying.

Scott's mum's sister, Julie, also moved in and I loved her. She's psychic and scarily accurate but also hilarious.

So there were a lot of us isolating together and for the first few weeks it was like a big commune and a bit of a novelty. Despite the fear and uncertainty about what was happening on the outside with this virus, we managed to rub along together quite well and we had some good laughs with each other.

But like many households during that time, the 'happy families' good vibes came under strain the longer the lockdown went on and there were frictions which started to surface. The first big stress for me came with my attempts to homeschool Matilda, which were a complete trainwreck from start to finish. Shortly after Scott was transferred to Preston, I'd enrolled Matilda in Westholme, the same school as I'd been to, and she'd started attending a couple of weeks before lockdown.

In Scotland, the school years run differently; children start later than in England and so she hadn't been due to begin reception up there until that coming August. On her first day at Westholme that March, she was with kids who had been in school since the previous September. Matilda had only ever been in nursery and so she was a little bit lost.

As was I. I'd never even heard of bloody phonics! It's not the way they taught kids to read when I was at school, so me and Scott didn't know our arses from our elbows about any of this. Talk about the blind leading the blind.

Anyway, a couple of weeks into the lockdown, I got a call from the school to ask why Matilda hadn't been joining the online classes.

Er, the what?

In the chaos of everything, I'd clearly missed the memo about virtual learning and I felt so guilty. I thought that all the teachers would think what a useless mother I was.

'Tell me everything I need and I'll make sure we're there in the morning!' I promised.

The school gave me all the details and links and the next day we got everything set up. We tried, my god we tried! But it was just diabolical. Matilda wouldn't sit still in a chair at all and when I thought about it later, why should she have? She was four, had never been to school, didn't know this teacher or what was being taught and I actually feel bad that we persisted with this farce for as long as we did.

There's no way kids that young should have been expected to attend lessons on a screen, what a spectacular waste of everyone's time.

That was one pressure in what was becoming a house of increasing tensions. Every day was groundhog day and we all started to get frustrated and snappy with each other. Me and Scott weren't getting on at all and if I'm honest, he'd pretty much stopped communicating with me on any level.

It was about mid-May and two months into the lockdown when I couldn't stand it any longer. There was an incident with his brother over the children where I felt Scott hadn't backed me up as he should have, so I packed the car, telling him I was going back to our apartment in Scotland. He could come with me or he could stay put.

'I'm staying,' he said.

'Right, suit yourself. That's it.'

I put the girls in the back and set off.

My agent Robin caught wind of what was happening and called to warn me I was going to get into serious trouble if I saw this plan through because it was against all the lockdown rules. I would be crossing a border and breaking the law.

'I don't give a fuck, Robin! I can't stay in that house a single minute more,' I said. 'I'm losing my mind. I have to get out.'

Robin suggested that I go to my parents' house instead and after a few deep breaths I agreed that this was a better option. It was less likely to land me in court, anyway.

At first I didn't tell Mum and Dad that I'd left Scott; I couldn't find the words. I just said me and the girls needed a breather from the over-crowding of the Sinclairs' house and to be fair to my parents, they didn't push me on that.

Scott was calling me and begging me to come back but I was determined it was finished.

'You've treated me like dirt, you stopped speaking to me and you never have my back. It's over, Scott. I'm coming up to 30 and I'm still dealing with this shit. I'm not doing it anymore.'

When I told my parents the truth, my dad was supportive, but my mum was upset because she was still Scott's number one fan. But even she put her arms around me and said it would be OK. They'd help me through whatever it was.

Over the next few weeks I spent some real quality time with my parents; we went for family strolls and I started to think about finding myself and the girls an apartment to rent nearby. There was a calmness that I'd not felt in a long time.

But then Scott turned up full of apologies and promising to change. He said he didn't want us to be over, he wanted us to be a family. I agreed to go for a walk and he spent the next hour saying that everything would be different if I gave him another chance.

I thought of the girls. I didn't want them to come from a broken home. I wanted to believe that we could make things work. Scott could always rope me back in. I was hopeless at resisting him.

To prove he was serious about starting again, Scott found a beautiful house for us in picturesque Edgworth in Lancashire and we moved there in time for Delilah's second birthday in June.

We were always better when we were just on our own and other people weren't involved, putting their two pennies in. I often thought that if me and Scott were ever going to work, we'd have been best moving to America and far away from any outside influences.

For the next six weeks everything felt… nice. Could we keep it like this? Peaceful, settled and with nothing to rock the boat?

Ummm.

I kind of knew before I even took the test. We'd been out for lunch at San Carlo in Manchester and I had absolutely stuffed my face like there was no tomorrow, I was that hungry.

'Steady on, Helen!' Scott had said. 'What's with the appetite?!'

And then there was the missed period. A telltale sign if ever there was one. I was so regular, my period would always start at 10am on the day it was due – you could quite literally set your watch by it. But it hadn't arrived as expected that morning.

Now I was looking at the positive pregnancy test. What the hell are you doing, Helen?

This wasn't a good time. We'd only just got back together, the relationship had been turbulent, we already had two kids, we still weren't married and I wasn't where I wanted to be in my career.

Before I even told Scott, I sent my best friend Jay a picture of me on the loo holding the test, with the word, 'Fuck.'

The truth is me and Scott weren't being careful enough, but I was shocked nonetheless. Although, weirdly, I remember feeling like I really, *really* wanted this baby. Maybe it was because I was about to turn 30 and was overanalysing my age, hearing the tick-tock of the biological clock. I honestly don't know but after the initial thunderbolt moment, I felt at ease with it.

The same couldn't be said for Scott. When I told him that night he was gutted.

'Fuck's sake, I don't want another baby, Helen! We've got enough on our plate with two.'

I hadn't been expecting him to be exactly delighted with the news, but the strength of his reaction knocked me. He was so pissed off.

'Well I *do* want this baby,' I said, in tears.

'It had better be a boy,' was all he said next.

With that, he took himself off and stewed on it for a few hours, trying to process the news. I left him to it, knowing that he needed the time on his own and once he calmed down and had recovered from the shock, he did come round to the idea.

In fact he was quite happy about it.

He put his arms around me. 'You know, I've always wanted three,' he said.

'Three's a good number,' I agreed.

'We'll make it work.'

I hoped so. Here we go again.

Chapter Ten

Beginning of the End

I KNEW THE SICKNESS WAS coming. It was a case of when, not if, and I spent the couple of weeks following the positive pregnancy test bracing myself for the inevitable onslaught.

Sure enough, it came on my 30th birthday (happy birthday to me, FFS) when Scott and I had travelled down to London for a couple of days to celebrate. We had dinner booked at Zuma, but I couldn't find it in me to eat any of it. It was like my appetite had been shot to pieces and I ended up having only a bowl of soup which I couldn't finish.

'It's starting, Scott,' I said, fully aware of what was about to hit me.

I woke up in the morning and, yep, that was it. As the HG bulldozed its way in, I was so poorly that I cried my eyes out on the train home because I knew only too well it was here to stay. Over the next few days the nausea came in waves and I tried as best I could to keep going. Scott had organised a really cute Harry Potter themed birthday party for me at home – it was just us and the girls and my mum and dad called round as well – but I couldn't touch a single thing from the buffet. Although I tried to smile through the party for the sake of Matilda and Delilah, and especially because I knew the effort Scott had made, I knew I was deteriorating.

From there the decline was rapid. So rapid that the next day my worried mum insisted on taking me to the GP where they tested my ketones and told us to go straight to hospital because I was at risk of liver damage.

This was, without doubt, the illest I'd ever felt in my entire life and I confided in the doctor that I didn't think I could carry on with the pregnancy if it was going to mean suffering like this for much longer.

Mum drove me to the hospital where I was admitted, the speed of the thing this time was astonishing. I was put on a drip to restore my fluid levels and given a sickness injection to stop the vomiting which was ghastly – when you're so weak and your whole body aches because you haven't eaten, the needle is an absolute killer. I had to lie in complete darkness because having the lights on would make me feel sick. That meant I couldn't watch TV either.

I felt dreadful from first thing in the morning to last thing at night with every ounce of life sucked out of me. I had zero energy, not even to brush my teeth.

After a couple of days, I was discharged, but that was

the first of many trips to the Royal Bolton over the next few months. I once had to change my pyjamas in the middle of the street *en route* to hospital because the bag I'd been throwing up into in the car had split and I was now covered in sick.

By then I'd lost all motivation, I didn't care about my dignity and nor did I have a shred of fight left in my body. I'd attend all appointments in my pyjamas and with my hair thick with grease from not being able to summon up the strength to wash it.

The hospital receptionist once unhelpfully said to me, 'Oh, hyperemesis gravidarum! I had that for nine months!' which was just about the worst thing anyone could have told me at that moment when I couldn't see a way out of the abject misery my life had become.

I was like the walking dead. This bastard of an illness eats away at your very core. It's like being allergic to being pregnant. The anti-sickness medication, which had worked quite effectively with Delilah, didn't seem to touch the sides this time.

You don't want to eat anything because you know you're just going to throw it all back up, but the more hungry you become, the worse the HG. I remember me and Scott went out for lunch one day while my mum took the girls for a couple of hours and I was crying in the car park because I felt too sick and weak to go into the restaurant. Encouraged by Scott, I eventually forced myself to go in.

'You need to eat, Helen,' he said. He was genuinely concerned about the amount of weight I was losing.

We ordered fish and chips which I managed to eat before throwing up the entire contents of my stomach all over the car park on the way out. Disheartening doesn't cover it.

I had to move in with my parents so they could look after me and the girls while Scott was training and playing. It was gut-wrenching for me hearing Delilah, who was only two, calling out for me, and it having to be my mum who went to comfort her.

'Where's Mummy, where's Mummy? I want Mummy...' And I would be in bed, throwing up through tears and tortured with guilt.

My mum was my rock during those weeks and she would sit and hold my hand through the worst of it. Scott would never have done that and I felt incredibly let down by him... during the worst of the HG he said something so shockingly stupid that I'm not sure I ever forgave him for it.

'If I had hyperemesis gravidarum,' he muttered, 'I'd just get on with it.'

Oh, would you now? How I'd have loved to reverse the roles even for five poxy minutes to see him bloody try.

I once asked him to bring me a drink of water and he said, 'Er, you're enjoying all this bossing me about.'

I didn't even have the energy to tell him to get fucked.

There wasn't anything about this I was 'enjoying'. I was broken.

I wish Scott had felt able to be more supportive. I just wanted a cuddle or someone to sit up in bed with me. He did that once, coming into the bedroom to watch Netflix on his laptop with a bowl of chicken soup, the smell of which made me spew my guts everywhere.

It was four and a half months before I started to feel better this time – halfway through the pregnancy – and I'll never forget the first meal I managed to keep down. It was a chili con carne my mum had made which I ate and then waited to be sick, only to find that it settled. The change in my energy levels from that one dinner was unbelievable.

The following morning I had breakfast and to my shock, I managed to keep that down, too. I dared to get in the car and drive to the shops and still didn't throw up, which, considering what I'd been contending with for the previous months, was a giant leap forward and a huge boost to my morale.

I wasn't 'cured' overnight and sometimes I'd be sick which would feel like a setback, but I took each meal as a baby step and across the next fortnight made brilliant progress. When I got to five months, I suddenly had a craving for red meat, which was the *weirdest* thing because I'd basically been a pescatarian for the last several years. But I was so low in iron, I was sure this was my body's way of repairing itself and therefore I couldn't ignore it. I had to devour a steak. The rarer the better!

To be fair to Scott, he stepped up and did all the cooking until I gave birth; his background is Jamaican Bajan and he's always been really good in the kitchen. But we were still having these stupid, petty little arguments which became big, blazing rows, often over the most trivial of things like him wanting to watch the boxing instead of sitting down to a Disney film with me and the girls. He just drove me around the bend as I'm sure I did him.

I knew deep down that we weren't strong enough as a couple to have this third baby and that was a scary place to be.

* * *

Scott loved the idea of sharing a birthday with his baby – he was born on March 25th – and so on the 24th (when I was one day overdue) we decided to take matters into our own hands to get things going. That meant having sex.

Apologies if this is TMI but it was hilarious because I was the size of a small country by this point, and trying to find a position where my mahoosive bump didn't cause a ridiculous obstruction was no mean feat! But we did it and something clearly worked because a few hours later I was in the bath having contractions. They became painful and frequent very quickly and I knew I had to get to hospital – when you've had two babies already, you kinda know the drill.

When we arrived at the Royal Bolton the staff were like, 'Ooh, Rosie from *Corrie*'s about to have a baby!' which me and Scott found quite amusing, and I was feeling relaxed about everything mainly thanks to the hypnotherapy sessions I'd had in the build-up to my due date with a wonderful birthing expert. She'd really prepped me in feeling calm and having the confidence in my body that it knew what it was doing and would do what it was supposed to. Even though my contractions were coming thick and fast, when I immersed myself in the water of the birthing pool, I felt strong and at ease with what needed to be done.

However, labour never fails to throw up a few surprises, does it? And when my waters didn't break, the midwives said they needed to pop them manually and – wow – that's when the pain went from 'significant but manageable' to 'oh my fucking god, kill me now.'

I can't even remember why now, but we were told I had to be transferred to a bed on the labour ward and Scott had to pick me up while I was screaming in agony and put me in a wheelchair. I was taken downstairs, wheeled through corridors while in the throes of labour as I tried to cover my face from the people noticing that here was 'Rosie from *Corrie*' wailing her head off. When we arrived at the room, Scott lifted me out of the chair and hoisted me onto the bed.

As well as my contractions, I was also now in extreme pain in my back thanks to a fall I'd had a week earlier when I'd gone to my mum's to collect Delilah. She'd excitedly run out onto the road when a car was coming, I'd grabbed her and pulled her back, but in doing so, slipped backwards mainly because I was wearing these idiotic Chanel sliders. I'd landed right in the tip of my coccyx.

My mum had taken me to hospital where they'd offered to induce me then and there, but I'd been determined to let labour happen naturally.

Because I was still feeling the effects of that fall, it meant I was going to have to give birth on my side but, after getting on to the bed, it was so quick and Charlie was born seven minutes later – just five hours after we'd arrived at the hospital.

And he'd managed to time his arrival to share his birthday with his dad as planned, although Scott was more busy being completely overjoyed that he finally had a son.

'It's a boy! I can't believe we've got a boy!'

I was elated too. Needless to say, I would have been happy with another little girl who I would have called Jemima – as long as they're healthy, that's all that matters.

But here Charlie was, the most handsome, perfect little boy I'd ever seen.

I was so blessed to have had the most kind and caring midwife to deliver him. She was like an angel. What midwives do is incredible, the way they look after you, woman to woman. What a gorgeous thing to do.

It had been a good labour inasmuch as it was straightforward but Jesus Christ, did I scream that hospital down during the final stages. If you took that last hour on its own, Charlie was my most painful of the three, but I'd never go as far as to say that I've had any bad birth experiences. I've been very lucky with all of them.

I wish you could bottle that feeling of the first few hours with your new baby, this little human who is going to be part of your world forever. There's nothing else like it.

I was in this beautiful dreamlike state, wrapped up in the blissful early moments of motherhood with no inkling of how quickly things were about to turn.

* * *

That first night, I took Charlie into the bed with me to breastfeed him. This was my third baby, so I was very confident about doing that, but a midwife popped her head in to check on us and she pulled me up on it.

'We're not allowed babies in the bed, love,' she said, gently.

She was very sweet with me but explained that it would be safer to move to the chair while Charlie finished his feed.

'You must be exhausted,' she said. 'How about you get some rest – I can take baby for a little while and you could have a sleep.'

My instinct was to say no thank you, I'd rather keep my baby with me. But she'd offered so kindly that, against my better judgement, I accepted and when I think about it now, perhaps my tiredness and battered body were working against me here.

Within five minutes of her taking Charlie, I started to feel anxious and my brain was going haywire. I got it into my head that the midwife was going to swap him with the baby of an Asian lady on the same ward and who I'd seen when I was in early labour. The Asian parents both had thick black hair like Charlie and the same skin tone and so it made sense that their baby could get mixed up with mine.

I rang the buzzer and the midwife came in.

'I really want my baby back,' I said.

'OK, love.'

I could feel the panic rising up.

'Now. I want my baby back now.'

They brought him back in but as they passed him to me, I couldn't be sure he was mine. I was staring at him, trying like crazy to see a family resemblance or to recall what the baby I'd handed over just a few minutes before looked like.

Were there any distinguishing features? How could I be sure?

In that small space of time – literally a few minutes – I'd gone from pure elation to being riddled with OCD. I started breastfeeding him and the only thing in my head was, 'This baby isn't mine. That midwife swapped him.'

My OCD was now in overdrive and any notion of

rational thinking was out the window. I'd tell myself to ignore the thoughts – I knew what this was, I'd been through a shitload of therapy, been there and got the T-shirt – but it was all just too powerful.

When I got home from the hospital the following day, I told Scott about what was happening in my head.

'I've got something to tell you. I'm worried that the midwife swapped our baby.'

'What do you mean swapped?'

'I don't think this is Charlie.'

'Huh?'

I told him how the midwife had taken Charlie and that in those few minutes must have switched him with the baby of the Asian lady.

'Come on, Helen. This is madness.'

'I know it's probably my OCD...'

'Do you reckon?' he said, rolling his eyes and not really taking seriously any of what I'd just shared.

'But I can't shake it, Scott. It's driving me insane.'

Scott is the most straightforward guy ever and everything is black or white with no grey areas. He doesn't understand mental health or emotions, so he wasn't being insensitive or dismissive with me, he just didn't get it.

But mind you, neither did he make much attempt (if any) to. My mum was always much better at supporting me through my worst episodes of mental health in a way Scott just couldn't. I wished he could understand it more... when you're in a serious relationship with someone and you have kids together, I think you need to be able to share your innermost fears with each other and know that you'll be listened to and heard.

I'd always tried to understand Scott's frustration with his football, his upbringing, his life and who he was as a person. He never really did the same in return and although there were many reasons as to why we eventually fell apart, I have to say that was one of the biggies.

I'll never forget the day he arrived back home from a 10-day pre-season trip with Preston in July. I was down in Surrey attending the wedding of my agent's daughter – Charlie was just a few months old and I'd been solo parenting while Scott had been away – and he FaceTimed me, really angry.

'Why is there no food in the fucking fridge?' he demanded. 'Is this a joke?'

That was the only thing he had to say to me. No consideration about the fact I'd been looking after three children, exclusively breastfeeding and battling postnatal depression on my own for the best part of two weeks.

I burst into tears and I remember speaking to his mum on the phone about it later only for her to back him up.

'Well, you could have got him some bread and milk, Helen,' she said. 'You never think of him.'

Postnatal depression and intrusive thoughts tightened their grip each day, dragging me deeper into darkness. I'd be breastfeeding Charlie while overcome with sadness because I yearned for the baby that I'd given birth to at the hospital.

My baby.

I miss that baby. That's my real baby. I should be breastfeeding him because he was mine. This baby doesn't belong to me.

I'm almost too ashamed to write this, but I want to be honest about it. Sometimes the thoughts would veer off into the most vile, racist thoughts which is not me at all – I'm vehemently anti-racist and obviously I have mixed race children.

Horrific.

I'm profoundly aware of the difficulties and prejudice they might face in life because of the colour of their skin. But I remember doing an interview for *Lorraine* with Ranvir Singh on a day when my OCD was particularly active and it was telling me I was going to say something racist live on TV.

You're going to say it and it's going to be horrendous. Your kids will be taken off you and your career will be over.

I was trying my utmost to get through this interview while these thoughts were crashing about in my brain the whole time and logically, *of course*, I'm never going to say those things, but in the moment, it feels vividly real and so frightening.

OCD plants the worst things you could possibly imagine inside your head and then makes sure you can't get them out. It had been telling me that if I was alone with Charlie I was going to do something stupid, and I'd been so scared of that happening. I would never have done anything, but my brain wouldn't accept that.

When the OCD started spiralling, that's the point I should have gone back into therapy. I knew the warning signs, but I let them go on because I thought I could try and fight it on my own, which clearly I couldn't.

It wasn't until Charlie was four weeks old that I admitted I needed help. This cruel condition was destroying me.

I travelled down to Birmingham to see Liz, the therapist who had helped me so much after Matilda and I broke down as soon as I saw her. I'd been hanging on for dear life for so long, it was as if a dam had just burst and once I started crying, I couldn't stop.

This was my rock bottom, but finally being able to talk about it to someone who was completely neutral, sharing exactly what was going on in my head and rationalising it was key to the start of my journey back to health.

So much of my OCD was wrapped up in shame, these thoughts were so repulsive that I hadn't been able to voice them to anyone. You create a hell in your head which feels completely real. It swallows you whole and controls you in every way, but saying it out loud, removes some of the power. And the more I talked, the easier it was to say to myself, 'OK, Helen, what the fuck was *that* about?!'

For the next three months, I went to see Liz every week and was very well supported by my mum in between –

she's always known exactly what to do when it comes to postnatal mental health.

Very gradually, the worst of it started to lift although I was left with quite a lot of anxiety and I'd become panicky, nervous and on edge about, seemingly, the silliest of things. I'd get worked up into a frenzy about stuff that had never bothered me in the past, and while I was fighting to get back to the person I was before all of this began, I couldn't find her.

It would take me a long time to do that.

Part of my recovery (and this is an ongoing process for me) has been about accepting that I am probably going to have spirals of OCD throughout my life and though I hope I won't, I know there's a possibility I'm going to feel that dreadful again. I'm prepared for that to happen. There are going to be times in my life where this thing cripples me, and as much as I wish my brain would just GTF, I'm stuck with it.

Sometimes I go for several months without doing anything at all, but then something will come into my head which is absolutely abhorrent, and I can't make it go away. But what I have confidence in now is that this is never a permanent state.

I will regain my peace because I refuse to let OCD win.

At the first sign of trouble, I see my therapist either in person or on FaceTime and I can release these thoughts into the open, we can sift through them and we can apply logic. This intrusive thought, whatever it is, and however sickening, is not the end of the world. It's not something which will ever come true and although a big part of my brain is telling me I'm not going to get through this, there's enough of it telling me that I can and will.

And I do.

I know how to deal with it now.

If medication works for other people then that's amazing – everyone is on their own journey and has to find the right path for them. But, for me, tablets just mask the problem.

Therapy, talking, self-care, sleeping and eating well, making sure my alcohol intake is on the right side of sensible, they all really help me.

I love being outside and that's good for my anxiety. I know this might sound a bit wanky, but being in nature and out in the countryside where I live, going for walks to clear my head, is so beneficial to me.

I write a lot of my thoughts down. I speak to people. I'm open about how I'm feeling. I share a fair bit on social media and I feel supported by the community I've built there.

I thought it might be helpful if I listed some prime examples of my OCD thoughts in one place. Compiling this and then seeing them all written down was hard for me, but I felt strongly it was important for this book and what I hope people will take from it.

Here goes...

- As a kid, as soon as I'd go into church the sexual thoughts would flare up
- I'd be convinced that I'd shit myself every time I'd do a reading at church with my parents sitting there, so proud. I'd dash to the loo afterwards to check my knickers, but my parents never questioned my routine
- When I was swimming I'd think maybe the pool was all an illusion and I was actually in the sea and going to be eaten by a shark
- I used to think I was adopted or perhaps that my older sister was actually my mum and my parents just took me in
- When driving in dark I'd think there was someone in the back of the car ready to knife me
- I'd also tell myself I'd run someone over and just blanked it out in horror, carried on driving and that I'd go to prison and never see my kids again
- When I was pregnant, I questioned if my babies were actually Scott's – what if I'd sex had with someone else and blanked it out?
- If Matilda didn't wear a certain babygrow, something bad would happen
- I thought I was going to die and would feel heartbroken at the prospect of leaving my baby motherless
- Friends holding my baby were going to give her infections
- Anyone I left my baby with was going to abuse her and she was too little to be able to tell me

- My baby becoming possessed and not being able to save her
- Me becoming possessed and stabbing my baby. I would hide knives before I went to bed
- I was worried I'd kill my baby in my sleep
- Not being able to wean my baby when I was alone because she was going to choke and die
- Constant worry in conversations about saying something awful and horrendous and everyone being like WTF?
- At *Corrie*, being scared I wouldn't say my lines and instead say something absolutely horrific which would shock everyone
- Saying something so dreadful, possibly even racist, in a live interview which would be career-ending
- Believing the midwife swapped Charlie with an Asian baby and missing the baby I'd given birth to
- Thinking I've killed someone but blanked it out
- Having to take pictures of every card or letter I've ever written as proof that I hadn't written something horrendous
- Thinking someone is in my house ready to kill me

* * *

Meanwhile, me and Scott were crumbling. When I'm stressed about something, I'd rather stab myself in the eye with a rusty fork than try to have a reasonable conversation about it with him.

The thing about Scott is that he loves our children with all his heart, and he's a fantastic dad in that respect, but he's never been into the whole spectrum of parenting. There was one Sunday when Matilda had a tutor coming to the house to help her with her maths. I'd taken all three kids swimming on my own and, as any mum will appreciate, that's flipping hard work! Getting them all changed at the start, wilting in the inhumane heat you get at public baths, trying to breastfeed Charlie, washing the girls' hair before leaving… it's A LOT.

I did all this while Scott was at home sat on his arse. Fair enough, everyone's entitled to an arse sit every so often, but when I got back, I told him that Matilda's tutor was arriving in 45 minutes and she'd need to use the kitchen for the lesson as the rest of the house was in chaos from being decorated.

Scott was watching the football in there and he was narked by the suggestion that he went elsewhere while Matilda was having her tutoring.

'Can't they just go in the playroom?' he said.

'No, because they need a table and chairs to work on, Scott! Are you seriously saying Matilda and the tutor need to sit on the floor in the playroom?'

He kicked up such a fuss about it that I look back at that day as being the beginning of the end. It was like a proper lightbulb moment for me and I lost some respect for him after that.

'Nope. You're not for me,' I thought. 'This isn't right.'

Certainly from that point, things went downhill, headed towards an unavoidable crash. Everything he did confirmed my belief that we were over, and made me more resolute in that conclusion. We went on a family holiday to Cornwall, staying in a beautiful hotel in idyllic surroundings, but Scott was moody the entire time. It was like he didn't want to be there. He made minimal effort with the kids and paid even less attention to me.

This half-arsed behaviour which I'd tolerated for so long was now completely tiresome, and I didn't want to put up with it anymore. As soon as we got home from Cornwall, he was off on his annual lads' holiday – going on his summer jolly with the boys was something he always made a priority even after we had children. Maybe that makes me sound quite needy and I had no reason to mistrust him, but he would be out of contact for most of that time away and could be quite cold when he came back.

Scott couldn't be the family man I wanted him to be. I couldn't help but compare him to my dad who's always been so family orientated and devoted to my mum. They are a team in every sense, and also happen to be madly in love.

Scott's just not like that and I was realising that he never would be.

There had been a time when I'd wanted nothing more than to marry him, but mainly due to the fact that he looked like he'd been shot every time I tried to bring up any kind of wedding plans, I'd let go of that fantasy some time ago.

We weren't aligned in our values or what we wanted family life to look like. It makes me upset even now, because all I ever wanted was to have my happy ever after and for that to be with Scott. But he pushed me to a point where I had no choice, and I had to stop kidding myself that this was ever going to work.

It was coming up to my 32nd birthday and I was thinking very seriously about what the rest of my life was going to be. I knew I was always going to love Scott, but I no longer felt loved back. If you spoke to Scott, I'm sure he'd tell you that I wasn't perfect either! I know I wasn't and there were definitely things I could have done differently or handled better over the years. But this relationship wasn't making me happy anymore. In fact, it was making me decidedly *un*happy.

The arguments were intolerable and I didn't want my kids around that sort of atmosphere. I'm super conscious that I'm my daughters' role model, and the thought of Matilda and Delilah growing up believing that rowing and crying and storming out were normal parts of a relationship was devastating to me.

I'd spend a lot of time with my little sister and her fiancé and they always had such a loving, balanced and healthy relationship. Mine was none of those things.

I could have stayed with Scott and had a really comfortable life materially, living in a six million pound house in Surrey and with all the shoes and handbags I'd ever wished for. But my children would have been raised witnessing a toxic relationship and unhealthy dynamics, and I hated that thought.

Although my mind was more or less settled on what I needed to do, we went on holiday as a family to Dubai for a fortnight that June, and I'd told myself to give it a chance. If there was anything to be salvaged, I should be open to it.

The first week was mostly fine and we got on, mainly because Scott got to chill out on a sun lounger all day. We met up with our Celtic friends, Sarah and Johnny Hayes, and had a brilliant time with them.

For the second week Scott said he wanted to fly his mum and dad out to join us. Now, I really like Scott's family and still get on well with his mum Sally, but I knew that idea wasn't the best one for our family holiday because the atmosphere would change.

His reasoning was that me and him would be able to spend more time together, but being around his family always put a pressure on us which is hard to explain. I also knew that as soon as his mum arrived as an extra pair of hands with the kids, Scott would take the opportunity to go and park himself on a sun lounger for the rest of the holiday.

I honestly think the main motivation for flying his parents over wasn't so that we got more time as a couple, it was to get him off the duties with the kids, knowing that me and his mum would manage it all between us.

Sure enough, after breakfast each morning, Scott and his dad would stay sitting at the table, chatting about football for two hours while I'd be down at the pool up to my eyes in floats, armbands and inflatables like a lunatic. Scott would eventually saunter over at about lunchtime.

Suddenly it wasn't *our* family holiday.

I've tried to understand the psychology behind it, and I know that Scott came from nothing and has always wanted to look after and take care of his parents and brothers. He's been a terrific son and sibling, but that was, at times, to the detriment of us.

Scott could never prioritise the family we'd created together.

We went out for dinner together at Billionaire in the Taj Hotel and I really made the effort, getting dressed up in this gorgeous Nadine Merabi dress and taking the time to do my hair and make-up.

Scott came in the room in a foul mood because he'd decided he wanted to watch the football instead of going out. There was no, 'Ah, Helen, you look nice,' just a load of moaning about how he was going to be missing some stupid match. He had a face on him the whole taxi ride to the restaurant, all the way through dinner, and then before we'd even finished our meals, he got up and said he was going to watch the game after all, leaving me sitting there on my own. I chased after him, but I knew at that moment it was 100 percent over.

I woke up the next morning and he was full of apologies.

HEAD & HEART

'I'm sorry for being a dick last night. I didn't mean to be like that. Can we just put it behind us?'

Well, no. Because I was worth more than that and there had to be more to life than this.

His words were empty and meant nothing to me.

I knew what I was going to do and this time there would be no turning back.

Chapter Eleven

Single Life

BREAKING UP WITH SCOTT WAS the hardest thing I've ever done and every single detail of the day is etched in my memory. There was a horrible, nervous feeling in my stomach that morning, knowing the conversation that lay ahead and after doing a food shop at Sainsbury's, I downed a couple of cans of gin and tonic for Dutch courage and then headed out on a bike ride to try and get into a good headspace.

When I got back, I asked him to sit down.

'Scott, I'm really not happy anymore. We can't carry on like this. I don't want to be with you. I don't want us to be together.'

I sat there in tears, but his reaction was so… matter of fact.

He was like, 'Fine, whatever.'

I actually don't think he thought for a second that I was

Good as gold: I was a bit of a goody two shoes growing up, never got in trouble and always followed the rules

Happy childhood: Growing up, I was always surrounded by lots of family who loved me

Dressing up: I love being a mum more than anything

Young parents: Neither me nor Scott had any idea how to even change a nappy. These days I could change 50 nappies in my sleep

Born broody: Ever since I was a little girl I've always wanted to be a young mum

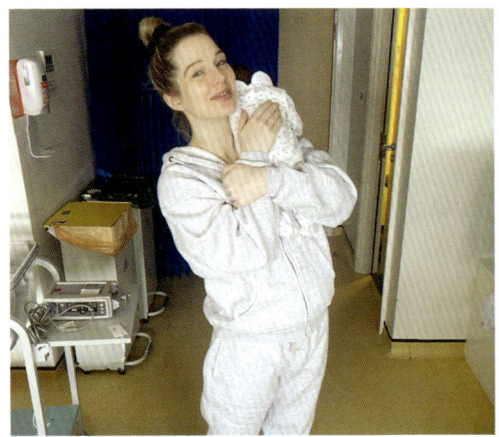 

Tough journeys: I struggled postnatally after Matilda and Charlie with OCD

A loving father: I really loved the kids' dad and all I wanted was my family

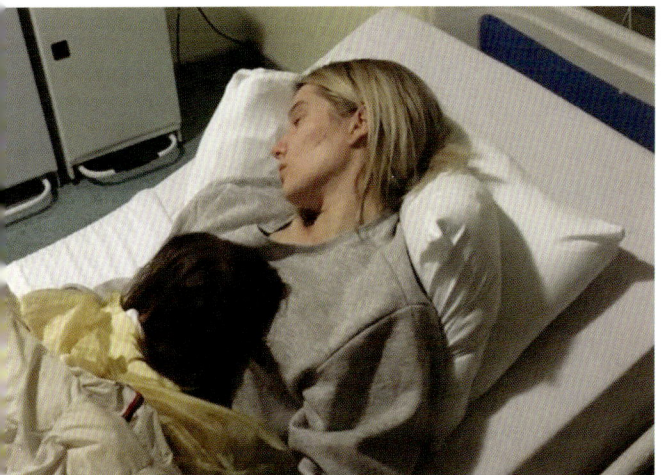

Hyperemesis Gravidarum: really took it out of me, I was hospitalised with Delilah and Charlie and had it three times

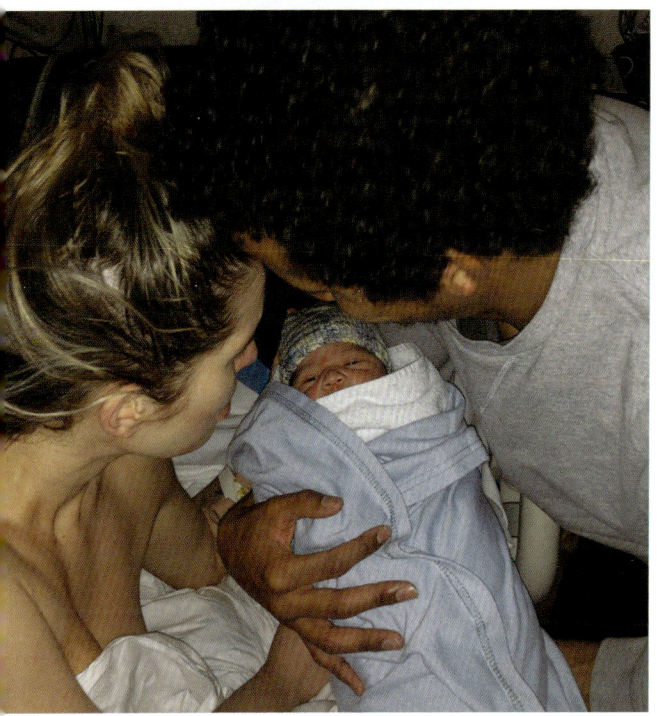

Postnatal OCD: After my first pregnancy, I felt like I was being suffocated by anxiety and intrusive thoughts. By the third, I wasn't scared of it, I knew how this thing worked and I had the tools and confidence to deal with it

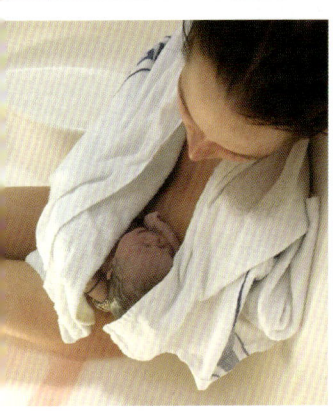
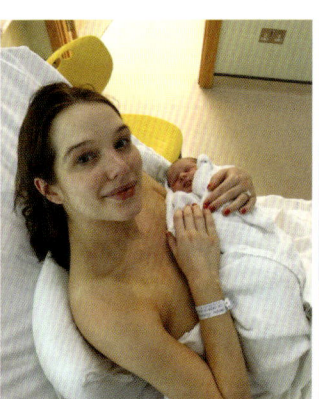
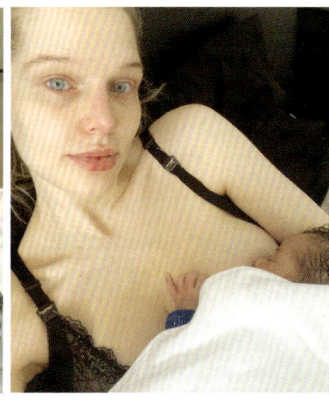

Love heals: The endless love I have for my three children gave me all the motivation I needed to get well again after some of the lowest times in my life. I don't know what I would do without them

Growing up happy: I live and breathe my kids and take every opportunity to show them how much I love them, whether it's holidays in Barbados or a Gruffalo party

Home away from home: I don't think I've ever been as settled as I was in Glasgow when Scott moved to Celtic. We were really happy there as a family

Robbie: Although I probably knew all along that he wasn't going to be my forever person, he did play an important role in my recovery and I'll always be grateful to him for that

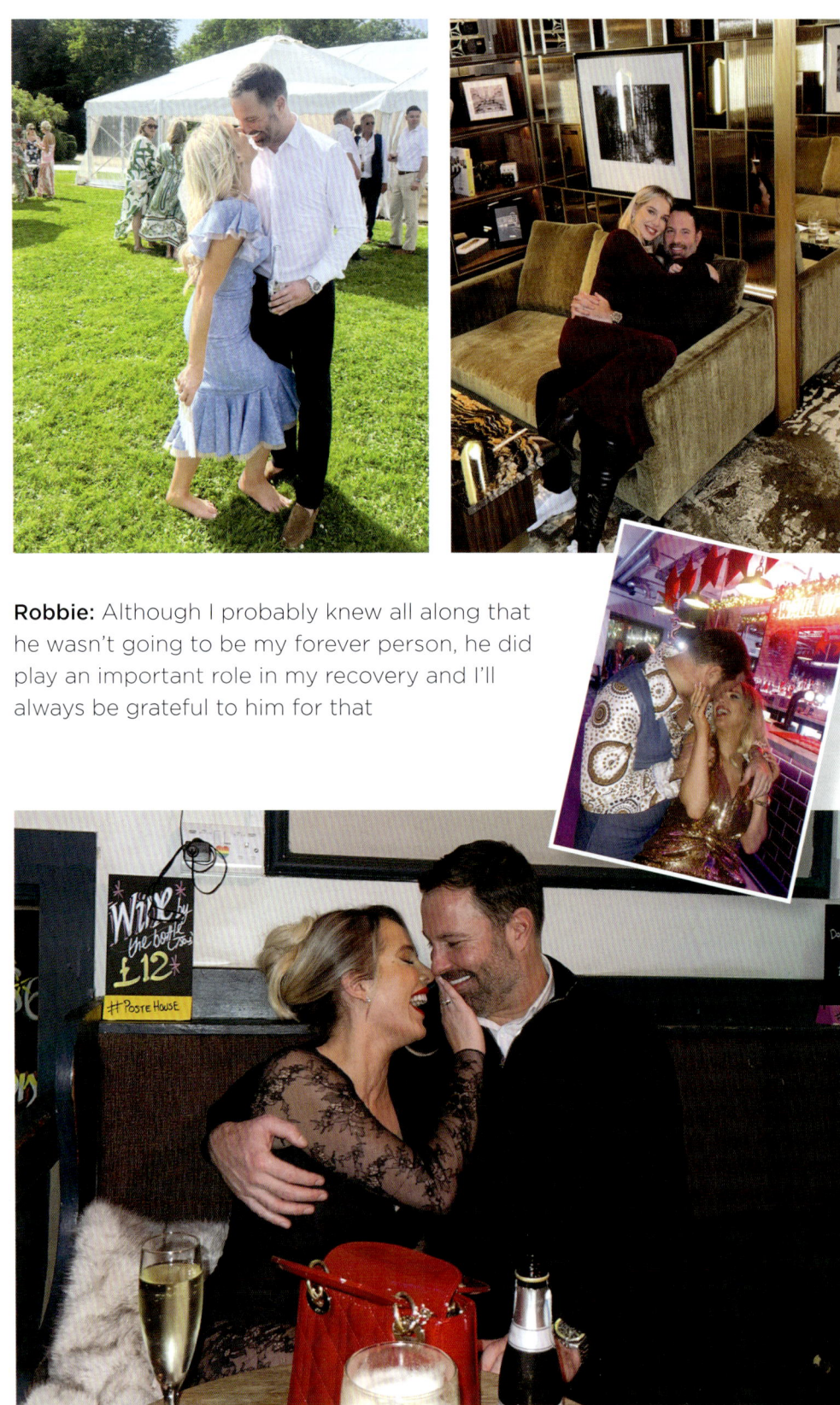

Outside court: Leaving Wirral Magistrates' Court

Mistakes were made: I adored David Haye, but it wasn't good for me. I wanted to change him and thought he would change for me

The father of my children: Scott will always remain a huge part of my life. We have three children together and, at one time, he was the love of my life. I can't simply 'unlove' him

The future: Despite the knockbacks, every day I count my blessings because I have so much to look forward to and to be grateful for

serious as he shrugged his shoulders and packed a bag. He went down to stay at his flat in London for a week and didn't check in with me and the kids once in that whole time. I was at home working and looking after the children and he couldn't be bothered to pick up the phone or FaceTime which, to me, spoke volumes.

In those days apart, my resolve only strengthened, and it was like the biggest weight had lifted off me. On my birthday a few weeks later, I went up to Scotland for a short break with my family and Scott wouldn't stop ringing me all day. Eventually I picked up and reiterated that my mind was made up and we were done.

I think that phone conversation was a penny-drop moment for him. Up until then, he'd assumed we'd get back together, just like we had in the past. I don't think he knew I had it in me to call time on it for real.

I'm not sure I'll ever meet anyone I love as much as I did Scott, but love isn't always enough. You have to be happy and secure with your partner and I hadn't been either of those things for a long time. I can't be in a relationship where I constantly have to 'cope' and not being Scott's girlfriend makes me healthier.

He couldn't love me how I wanted him to love me and that was a really hard truth to swallow because it meant I had to let go of a dream I'd been clinging on to. That was incredibly painful, but that has made me so much stronger as a person.

I gave that relationship all I could. For the sake of our

children, I tried everything to make it work and so I have no regrets, but Scott got too safe, thinking I'd never leave him.

In terms of how my future looked, I hadn't thought too far ahead. My only plan was to carry on working as much as I could, and I knew I had a decent amount of savings to support me and the kids. At that time, I felt financially secure.

Scott and I continued to live under the same roof although we were very much separated and barely saw each other. He'd been released by Preston and was looking for a new club and would take himself off to London. On the days he was back, I'd make sure I had work that took me away or meant that we weren't getting under each other's feet, but I can't pretend that it wasn't a strain because there were times when you could have cut the tension with a knife.

So when an opportunity to take part in an 'all star' version of *I'm a Celebrity...!* which would be filmed in South Africa and feature a cast of memorable campmates from previous series, I grabbed it with both hands.

Not only would it give me a break from the troubles at home, but the idea of going back in there a decade on from my first stint, and having the chance to redeem myself was a really strong pull.

Back in 2012, I had been young, naïve and not in the right mindset to be on the show and as a result, I'd embarrassed myself. I wanted to prove that there was more to me than being a scaredy cat.

I was so serious about going back and this time smashing it, I put myself through a makeshift *I'm a Celebrity...!* boot camp before I left for South Africa. I went to my local Go Ape to try and conquer my fear of heights and although I cried as I climbed up the ladders to reach the nail-biting ziplines, I was determined to do this. I went there so many times in the weeks leading up to South Africa it was an actual joke. They should have given me a discount for being their customer of the year!

The more I went, the easier the heights got and combined with a bit of hypnotherapy, my fears started to dissipate. My agent also found me a guy who does creepy crawly birthday parties for kids and I went along to meet him where he introduced me to his collection of bugs, snakes and spiders, and set me a challenge not to scream as he placed them on me.

It was brutal at first, but once I'd trained myself to keep the panic at bay, I started to get desensitised and the rational part of my brain told me these creatures wouldn't hurt me.

They were just on my skin and it might not be a particularly nice sensation, but nothing bad was going to happen.

I also needed to tackle my issue with rats as I knew there was every chance I'd be coming face to face with those little horrors again, so I arranged with the retail store

Pets at Home to pop into a branch and hold one. Again, not the most enjoyable way to spend an afternoon, and I definitely wasn't tempted to bring one home as a pet, but it helped ease my anxieties, and by the time I was on the flight to South Africa in September, I was feeling quietly confident about whatever lay ahead.

And, even if I do say so myself, I nailed it. The show was being pre-recorded and would air the following year, so there was no public vote involved at any stage and that meant the trials were evenly spread out among all the celebs. I didn't shirk any of them and the real turning point came with one called World's End, which saw me, Amir Khan and Myleene Klass climbing a 1,100m high crane-like structure suspended over a sheer drop to unhook stars and win meals for camp. I barely flinched!

When the series went out in April 2023, it was lovely to see so many people posting positive comments about my efforts, some even declaring me a 'new woman'! In many ways, that's exactly what I was.

I made some beautiful friendships in the camp and especially loved Jordan Banjo who finished runner-up. He's so funny and is fab company. I was *obsessed* with Carol Vorderman. I want to be like her when I eventually grow up; she's so confident, strong and free. We'd have chats about her single life and it sounded huge amounts of fun which gave me a bit of hope and inspiration for my own future.

Georgia 'Toff' Toffolo was hilarious and I really liked Joe

Swash and Amir Khan, too. Dean Gaffney was amazing and while I know Gillian McKeith has a bit of a reputation for being an oddball (I think after her original series in 2010 she came out even more hated by the public than me!), I thought she was cute. She really made an effort to be friends with me and I found that so sweet.

The only one I perhaps didn't have quite as much in common with was Myleene. She is absolutely stunning and a very talented lady, but we're different people, and I have no idea how she manages to do as much as she does. She was always really nice to me but she's such a powerhouse, I always felt a bit, I don't know… inadequate compared to her.

A major positive for me was making peace with Ant and Dec. I reckon they were fully expecting a repeat performance of 2012 with me getting my knickers in a twist at the slightest hint of a cockroach, but I went in there and stormed it and they appreciated that.

I lasted until day 12 when me and Dean lost the Crate Escape survival trial, but I'd given everything my best shot and felt so proud of myself. When I came back to the UK, I was in such a healthy frame of mind and that helped further distract me from the aftermath and fallout of my split from Scott.

Finally, I was on the right path and things were looking up.

* * *

Scott had been without a football club since Preston released him at the end of the 2021-22 season and was looking for a fresh contract elsewhere. But it was still a big shock when he announced in October he was signing for Bristol Rovers which was a three-and-a-half-hour drive from where we lived in Bolton, the area our children were settled and went to school.

Of course, I understood that footballers go where the work is, and I knew how desperate he was to play again, but I struggled with his decision to uproot himself and move quite so far away. We might not have been together anymore, but we still had children to take care of and co-parent.

I knew this would effectively make me the sole carer because how could he possibly help with the day to day of family life from 200 miles away? How often was he realistically going to see his children?

I asked him if there wasn't a club nearer, who would take him on. He said he had no choice, but I'm sorry, there are always choices in life and to me, he'd chosen to ignore his responsibilities as a parent, safe in the knowledge that I'd be there to pick up the slack.

Everything – and I mean everything – would now be left to me to manage and juggle because his training and playing schedule would mean he wasn't able to come and see the children even once a week.

In short, I was fuming. And let down, again.

Scott's plan was to move into the house in Bath he'd

bought for his parents and where his brother and his family were still living, so he was going to see more of his niece and nephew than he was his own kids.

Him being so far away was hard on the children and Matilda especially missed her daddy. I would always have his back, even if I had to do it through gritted teeth because I never wanted the kids to think badly of Scott or to get in between the issues we had with each other.

'Daddy loves you so much,' I'd assure them. 'He just has to work really hard for the pennies so you can live in a lovely house.'

Matilda has always had this astonishing level of emotional maturity and even though she was only seven when me and Scott split up, the way she processed and understood it was unbelievable.

There was one day we were in the car – she was in the front with me, and Delilah and Charlie were in the back.

I said, 'You know Mummy and Daddy are just friends now, don't you? We're not going to be boyfriend and girlfriend anymore. I still love your daddy and he still loves me, but we're just going to be friends instead.'

And she said, 'Is that because you're not compatible?'

Wow.

'Yeah, I guess that's it, darling.'

She did ask a few times if we were getting back together, and I was always honest with her that we were better as friends while secretly thinking, 'Do you honestly want me to be miserable for the rest of my life?!'.

Matilda also said something which really struck a chord, an observation I thought was so revealing.

'Mummy,' she said, 'when you were boyfriend and girlfriend, I never saw you and Daddy cuddle or kiss.'

I thought that was so sad, because me and Scott were still a young couple and we should have been quite lovey-dovey and yet, she'd never noticed us being affectionate with each other.

A few days after Scott moved to Bristol Rovers, I was on the train down to London where I was attending the *Daily Mirror*'s Pride of Britain Awards that night when my agent Robin called me.

'Helen, the papers have the story that you and Scott have separated. Obviously, you're not wearing your engagement ring and that will be noticed on the red carpet tonight… but do you want me to stop the story?'

I thought about it for a few seconds and then said to go ahead and confirm. Let them run it. In my heart it felt like the right time to take that step and go public.

I knew that the story would be running as I got ready to go to the awards, and although I was a little nervous about what the coverage might look like, and how people would respond to it, I was at peace with making the break-up official.

I was also looking forward to Pride of Britain which I was going to with Brooke Vincent, because it was always a fantastic night full of emotion and brilliant people. And this particular year it would see me bump into a certain someone from my past. Someone who would go on to have a major impact on my future.

David Haye.

* * *

Before I get into this, I have to emphasise that the thought of playing the dating game again had never even entered my mind. It simply wasn't on my agenda, and so even though he was looking fit, when David came up on stage to present an award, my first thought was only about how lovely he'd been to me in the jungle 10 years before.

My second thought was, 'Oh fuck, I blocked him after that and I hope he doesn't remember!'. If he did, he didn't mention it. When Brooke and I headed to the bar afterwards, David was there with a few women hanging off him (obvs) so I went over to say hello. I had no flirty intentions, I just thought it would be nice to have a chat and the two of us had a good catch up about life since *I'm a Celebrity…* He asked if I was still with Scott, and I told him we'd recently split up and that was about as far as the conversation went.

But later that night, I DMd him a photo of us which had been taken at the awards.

'Lovely to see you, David. You were always so kind to me in the jungle. Lots of love. PS I look like your fan in this pic!'

He messaged straight back.

'Really good to see you. Send me your WhatsApp number.'

Argh! Instantly I was like, 'Ohhh no…' because I knew that meant he wanted to take things up a notch and I just couldn't do it. I still felt loyal to Scott, I wasn't anywhere near ready to get into anything else with another man, even casually.

So, I ignored this message and left it, telling myself that if I still liked him by Christmas, I could DM him then. Don't ask me what logic I was applying to this timeframe because there was no logic involved whatsoever – I was so new to dating and completely out of touch with how things worked.

As it happened, I still had zero interest in men by the December. I hadn't even felt a stir. All I did was look after the kids, renovate the house and work, but David randomly popped up on my Insta feed because he was on this eight-week fitness plan and I thought I might as well drop him a message.

'I never sent you my number after Pride of Britain, so sorry,' I wrote. 'Are you OK? How's your 'fat to fit' going?'

But he never replied and I didn't give it any more thought after that. I certainly wasn't going to pursue him, heaven forbid! That, I assumed, was that.

Then in January came news about David's 'throuple' situation which meant he and his long-term partner Sian Osborne were openly navigating a polyamorous relationship. When it emerged that Una Healy from The Saturdays was apparently the 'other woman' I think it took everyone by complete surprise. The story was all over the papers and was massive showbiz news, everyone was obsessed.

For the record, Una has since become a good friend of mine and I love her – I think we've bonded over our respective fucked up experiences with David, which you'll hear more about later, and she's been a huge support to me as I've recovered from everything that happened next.

But seeing the picture of the three of them together, Una and Sian on David's arms like his trophies, was the weirdest thing, and all my friends who knew I'd had some contact with him were messaging, laughing their heads off that it could have been me.

Mentally, I put David away in a little box marked: Don't even go there.

* * *

At the start of the new year, I'd found myself quite restless. I couldn't put my finger on what was bugging me, but there was nothing I wanted to watch on telly, nothing I wanted to eat in the fridge and my overwhelming feeling was one of loneliness.

On Valentine's Day I went out for a drink with a friend who's really happily married and I opened up to her about this nothingness, this flatness, I felt engulfed by and as we chatted, it dawned on me that I was probably sexually frustrated.

I'd not had sex since splitting up with Scott about eight months before, and that was something now glaringly missing from my life. To go from having regular sex for 13 years to absolutely zilch… that's got to have an effect and I thought, 'Come on, Helen, you're only 32, you're single and you should probably do something about this!'

At that point I'd only slept with four people – the two one night stands when I was 16 and then my two boyfriends, Danny and Scott. It felt like I had a bit of catching up to do.

So, I got to work.

The first thing I did was get on Raya, the exclusive dating app for people in the public eye, and I got a fair bit of attention very quickly which was hilarious, suddenly having all these men trying to pull me. Me and my friend were *howling* as we swiped through the app and especially because the picture I'd used for my profile had been taken when I was pregnant. But it was nice getting noticed out of nowhere because Scott had looked at me as part of the furniture for so long.

I'd get ridiculously over-excited if someone messaged me. A top TV star who I won't name here, got in touch messaging, 'You're my dream woman,' and purely for banter I sent him a picture of me in a little pink Easter bunny outfit from a campaign I'd just shot for Ann Summers.

He wasn't my type in the slightest, so I didn't set up a

date, but I found our interactions really funny. The whole thing was such an eye-opener for me – this was a completely different dating world to the one I'd left behind when I got together with Scott back in 2009, long before the apps had taken off.

It was all boosting my confidence which had been quite low up to that point. I'd also just had my boobs done and was feeling quite good about the way I looked for the first time in a while. My boobs had been so saggy after pregnancy and breastfeeding and I'd been left with a lot of excess skin. Whenever me and Scott had had sex I'd always kept my bra on because I was self-conscious even with him.

I've never once regretted getting them done and I don't think I would have felt able to date if I hadn't.

Not every interaction was welcome though. The controversial influencer and male supremacist Andrew Tate slid into my DMs with a message saying 'Sons?' alongside a heart emoji. I was shocked but then I laughed. And before you ask, no of course I didn't reply!

There was one guy, a well-known actor, who came up on my social media doing a reel for a brand and I thought, 'God, he's so handsome...'

I'd met him years before on a job and we'd had a little flirt back then, but I was with Scott at the time and so it hadn't gone any further than a bit of joking around. Anyway, I liked his reel, followed him, and he messaged me straightaway.

We started DMing each other quite a lot over the next few days which was a game-changer for me because I'd never had this sort of experience with anyone before and I got properly into this guy. After a couple of weeks, I bit the bullet and asked if he wanted to meet up in London. And you know what? The pillock blew me out! He said he couldn't come because he was 'too busy.'

It had been fun while it lasted, but he clearly didn't want to take it beyond the DMs. My friend said, 'Helen, you're so sex starved, you'd have had him for breakfast! He had a lucky escape.'

She called me a man-eater which I thought was a bit harsh but I was definitely more than ready for a bit of action.

And that's when David came back on the scene.

When the Ann Summers pictures (which I'd shot in my pink utility room of all places) were splashed across the papers, he messaged me out of the blue saying, 'Wow, you look so hot…'

That started a bit of back and forth and I asked him if he still had a girlfriend. He said he did, but that it was an open relationship.

For me, that was a no-no – I was flattered by his attention but would never do anything to hurt another girl – and so I tried to take a step back. He persisted, asking me lots of questions on whether I'd found anyone else since Scott and I told him I hadn't.

'You're a classy queen,' he replied.

WTF?!

We continued messaging over the Easter holidays, and it was while I was on holiday in Dubai with the kids and my friend that something clicked. It was a beautiful night and I suddenly had a moment of clarity.

I was always such a *good* girl. I did everything right; pleased my mum, pleased my dad, played by the rules. If I fancied this guy, why shouldn't I have a night with him and be done with it? He had an open relationship, she would know about it, so how would I be doing anything wrong?

Fuck it.

Before I could talk myself out of it, I texted David. I told him that the kids were going to be at their dad's the following week and I was staying for a couple of nights in a hotel in London – he was welcome to join me.

'That sounds lovely,' he replied. 'We'll go somewhere for dinner.'

'No! I'm not being seen anywhere with you! Just come to my room.'

I thought I'd just have one night with him, get him out of my system, that'll be done, move on with your life, Flanagan.

Ha, ha bloody ha.

Chapter Twelve

Love Struck

BEFORE I CAUGHT THE TRAIN down to London, my best friend Ashley came to the house and got me dolled up. As well as being my make-up artist, she's also like a second older sister to me, and I know now she was worried about what I was getting into.

David is a walking, talking red flag whose reputation goes before him, but she didn't want to ruin my excitement.

'Just be careful, Helen,' she said as she dropped me off at the station.

I felt all fluttery on the way down, but I was looking forward to having a good night with a man I'd fancied for years – the kids were with Scott and his mum, so they were safe and this was my time.

When David knocked on my hotel room door, I answered it wearing a cute little blue pyjama set. He had sunglasses on and looked gorgeous, but it was a bit awkward at first and I'm sure he was slightly nervous, too.

We had a drink and started to talk. He was nice to be around, he was charming and full of compliments and eventually we went to bed together. As a woman, I'd been wanting to experience a sexual connection with somebody and David gave me that.

We had an amazing night and I went to sleep in his arms feeling pretty wonderful. He'd held me and kissed me and had made me feel like I was the most beautiful girl in the world. But there was a rude awakening the next morning when he told me that his girlfriend was outside the hotel waiting for him. She kept on ringing his phone and although he was respectful with me, checking that I was OK and saying he'd loved spending time with me, he dashed off quite quickly.

It was all a bit deflating, but he messaged me throughout the morning and we continued to communicate as I flew out to do a bikini shoot in Spain. I sent him some of the pictures from that which he liked, and I asked if we could meet again at the hotel when I was back in London the following evening.

We spent another night together – it was sexy, exciting and all the things I'd been missing since being single.

Over the next couple of months, we met up in that same hotel several times and as time went on, I started to get a bit more daring, venturing out in public for walks and food together – this was in central London so how we never got papped is beyond me.

Admittedly, I started getting feelings for him early on. Very real feelings. I think sex often means something deeper to women and if you're regularly sleeping with a guy it's difficult not to fall for them. That's certainly the case for me.

But David always had his girlfriend Sian, and I knew there was never any chance of us being exclusive because that wasn't how he operated. I was also adamant that I wasn't going to join the throuple, despite his best efforts to recruit me. He'd frequently ask if I would meet Sian, but I always said I didn't feel comfortable with that idea.

The second time I slept with him he'd said, 'Now you're part of the team.'

Er, no. I definitely was not part of 'the team'. I'm not a prude, but I've never been into that – it was David I liked, I didn't have any interest in Sian, beautiful though she is.

He kept on trying, though.

In the middle of May there was a big boxing match at Wembley Arena – David's good mate Joe Fournier was taking on the musician and influencer KSI and I was really keen to go. David said he'd sort me out with some tickets and that we'd hang out at Joe's after party.

'It'll be fun,' he said. 'Sian is really excited to meet you.'

Eek. That was the first I knew of Sian being there too and I thought it was quite unbelievable that she was apparently looking forward to meeting me since I was the 'other woman', but I put any misgivings to one side because I was so mad on David.

The night of the fight, I wore a sexy little corseted leather dress from Agent Provocateur and headed to the arena where I was sitting quite near the front with a mate of David's and his partner, a girl who has since become a really good friend to me. So there were some silver linings from this whole thing.

David was ringside with Sian and his daughter, and when I spotted them, I suddenly felt extremely awkward and wondered what I'd been thinking coming here. He came over to say hello, giving me a hug and a kiss on the cheek.

My life had always been quite wholesome and this felt seedy and wrong – a few days before I'd been out for a coffee with a good friend who I'd poured my heart out to and she'd said, 'Oh my God, Helen, you're the side chick!'

I was so naïve I didn't even know what that meant. A side chick is a woman who is involved with a man already in a committed relationship with someone else. The dirty little secret.

'Helen, you of all people should not be the side chick,' she'd told me. 'You should be the main event.'

I bumped into the *EastEnders*' actress Jacqueline Jossa at the bar. I'd always got on with her and so confided in her about the situation with David because I was feeling so self-conscious. I don't think she was impressed. She was a bit like, 'Helen, what are you doing?' which, to be fair, was a very good question.

What *was* I doing? What had I done?

After the fight (which was won by KSI, not that I'd been paying much attention because my mind was very much elsewhere) Sian approached me and honestly, she was the most beautiful girl I'd ever seen.

No pictures can do justice to what she's like in the flesh; she's completely breathtaking. We got chatting and although I felt nervous because this was such a ridiculous predicament, she was nice to me and everything seemed friendly.

Then David joined us and said to Sian, 'She's hot, isn't she?' nodding towards me which was so cringe and made me want the ground to swallow me whole.

The Helen of today would have got the hell out of there. Whether Sian was OK about me and David or not, she deserved so much better than this, and there have been many times since that I've wished I could say to the girl, 'I am so sorry for what I did to you. I was messed up at the time, I didn't know what I was getting into and I feel terrible.'

I know that she probably wouldn't thank me for it, but I truly regret being part of the circus. I've not got a bad word to say about Sian. I hope she's OK.

There was a small post-fight drinks party arranged for Joe at a London hotel and somehow I ended up travelling there in the back of David's car with him driving and Sian in the passenger seat.

Worst. Journey. Ever.

Sian is a 6ft supermodel and David is 6ft 4in and almost as broad, so it was as if they were my parents and I was the little child. For the millionth time that night, I questioned my sanity.

When we arrived at the hotel, I really didn't want to go in because it was just so weird, but David gave me a cuddle and encouraged me inside. It was a nice crowd and everyone made me feel welcome and yet I couldn't shake the discomfort – everything about the scenario was surreal. At one point I found myself with Sian while David sat in between us scoffing crisps, and I couldn't comprehend how it had come to this.

I think his plan had possibly been to get me and Sian involved in a threesome that night, but when I made it clear that wasn't going to happen, he told her that he was 'just going to take Helen home'.

I couldn't look at her as we left. I hate now that I was part of that, this betrayal of the sisterhood, but I was blinded by my obsession with David who had me wrapped around his little finger. I think I gave Sian a hug as me and David were leaving and once we were in the car, I told him this had to be our last night together because the guilt was too much.

He started to get really tearful about the thought of us not seeing each other anymore and that pulled at my heart – he knew exactly what to do to win me back round.

We went back to my hotel and spent the night together, but I still felt terrible the next day. It was so strange because I was guilty about Sian but also envious of her – not only was she stunning but she also had David. She was the one he was devoted to, I was just the bit on the side.

* * *

There were a few early warning signs that there was another side to David and I felt some of his behaviour could spill over into possessiveness. He was prone to jealousy, and made it clear he didn't want me to see or speak to any other men. He'd tell me how much he hated 'slags' and that he wanted me just to himself.

I thought I was in love with him, but some of the things he said made me feel uneasy and I knew at the back of my mind that whatever we had between us probably wasn't going to end well and it needed to stop.

Not long after the Fournier fight and about two months into our relationship, we met at our usual hotel and I told him how I felt.

'I really appreciate you being here for me, David, and I think a lot of you, but you've got a girlfriend and this isn't going to work for me. I want to be free to date other people and see who might be out there for me.'

I thought I'd explained the situation really well and that he would say something like, 'We've had a nice time together, I think you're a great girl and I understand why you feel that way.'

He was 10 years older than me, so I expected him to respond as a mature adult. But what I said went down so badly and he instantly turned cold. He wouldn't touch me; he could barely even bring himself to look at me, it was like I disgusted him. I don't think David is used to women saying no to him.

Because of the horrible shift in atmosphere, I became upset and started to cry.

'I expect perfection from you,' he said. 'Why are you speaking to me like this? Did you speak to Scott like this? No wonder he left you. You do not speak to me in this way.'

He was seething. I felt like I couldn't breathe. I couldn't equate the man who had been so kind, romantic and loving with the one who was so angry with me now. I cried the whole way back to Bolton on the train and felt utterly worthless.

It didn't help that I'd started drinking quite heavily as well – most evenings I'd have a bottle of wine and this would only worsen my mood and further batter my self-esteem.

I hadn't wanted it to end this way. I was devastated that he seemed to hate me so much. I can see now that he had me completely under his control because rather than blocking his number and running for the hills, I found myself longing to get back with him.

My confidence was on the floor.

So, after a couple of weeks when David started messaging me saying that he missed me, I was ecstatic. He said he'd come and see me at my house and that he'd checked with Sian who was fine with it.

Hook, line and sinker.

I arranged a night of childcare and a couple of days later, David travelled up by train and I collected him at Manchester Piccadilly.

We had a really lovely night together, it was very chilled and he was super affectionate. I thought everything was 'fixed' between us, but the next morning he turned again.

'I need to go back to London,' he announced, offering no explanation as to why he was dashing off so quickly, but making it clear there was no point in trying to change his mind.

'OK, babe,' I said, pulling on some joggers. 'I'll take you back to the station.'

He was so frosty in the car all the way to Manchester and it put me on edge because I had no idea what I'd done wrong or why he'd had this personality transplant overnight. When we got to Piccadilly, I suggested we go to Starbucks while he waited for his train, and he seemed to warm up a bit after that, he was chatting to me at least.

But then he did something which was so bizarre it knocked me sideways and I still don't know what he was playing at. He started telling me about a girl who was quite obsessed with him and who he'd had to 'let go'.

I couldn't work out where this was going.

'Did you know she went on a date with Scott?' he said, expressionless.

I started to feel a bit sick because Scott's love life was not something I was ready to hear about.

'Oh, OK,' I said.

'Yeah, how weird is that?' he replied, now smirking. 'She went out with Scott, but she's obsessed with me!'

And then he made a point of showing me a picture of her.

'Gosh, she's beautiful...' I said, not knowing how else to respond. 'But that's making me feel a bit strange, can we change the subject?'

'Sure, I need to go and get my train anyway.'

We walked towards his platform and he kissed me goodbye, but then he looked at me in a way which is very difficult to describe, but was so unnerving that I nearly dropped my coffee.

Why was he looking at me like that?

I rang him later and asked if he was OK – he said he was fine but in a very moody tone, and in my head I started to question everything about his trip north to see me. On reflection, I think I'd pricked his ego by saying I wanted to be free to see other people, and he'd decided to mess with me in return.

It was like revenge: he'd give me a really romantic night

and then snatch it all away again in the morning by leaving in a rush and dropping this bombshell about the other girl.

I truly believe that the only reason he came to the house was to hurt me.

He later posted something on his Insta stories about being on a 'hot date' alongside a photograph of the same girl he'd shown me the picture of. It was like he was taunting me.

I should have just left it. Walk away, Helen. Stop falling into his traps.

But I messaged him and asked, 'Is this the girl that you told me went on the date with Scott?'

'Yeah, she's really sweet. It's not a big deal, babe,' came the reply.

I told him I didn't feel very well and then he phoned me saying he was sorry and that he 'hadn't meant to upset you, baby.'

After that, he started regularly messaging and FaceTiming me and he reeled me in again. Everything about my mood was linked to David. When I was happy, it was because things were going well with him. If I was depressed, it was because things were dreadful. It was like he controlled all my emotions.

I once posted a TikTok about dating experiences as a single mum, and he went ballistic about that. I was so under the thumb that I took the video down, apologised for upsetting him and promised to check with him before I posted anything else.

When I write all this down now, it seems mad that I went along with this for so long, but I always felt like I could be the girl who was able to change him. He'd opened up to me about things in his past and I felt honoured that he'd trusted me to do that. I thought I understood why he was the way he was and that I could help him.

I even believed for a while that he might even leave Sian for me, especially when he told me that he loved me for the first time. That was in September, the night before the National Television Awards, and it meant everything because I was besotted with him. He even started talking about wanting a baby together.

But I was also unsure about how to take his words because how could he love me when he still had a girlfriend? And sometimes we'd spend the night together and he wouldn't even message the next day to check I'd got home safely – were those the actions of someone who was in love?

I could feel my mental health sinking because David and our relationship consumed me.

I wanted to have a week when we didn't speak to see if I could clear my head and figure out what to do, so I had a phone conversation with him and said I thought we should have some space because I could sense this wasn't good for me right now.

But he had such a hold over me that within about three days I was pining for him and so I sent a message saying how much I missed him. He called me, and when

I answered, I thought he was going to tell me he missed me too. But instead, he unleashed this rage down the phone.

'Do you think this is funny? Do you think you can fucking message me after you won't speak to me? You're gonna have a taste of your own medicine now. Who do you think you are? You've been shagging someone else's boyfriend for the last six months – how do you think that's made Sian feel?! What kind of woman are you?'

This is after he'd told me the whole time that Sian was completely cool with it because they had an open relationship.

I was shattered.

I had to go to London for a couple of jobs, but in the morning it was like I couldn't even get out of bed; I was so depressed and lifeless. I had to drag myself out the room.

This was October and David's birthday was coming up, so I bought him a trinity bracelet from Cartier and left it with the concierge at the hotel he stays in.

As I was driving home, he called me.

'Babe, I really can't accept what you've given me.'

'It's fine, I want you to have it. Please take it.'

I just wanted him to have something from me.

'I can't take it. All I want from you is your body, that's enough for me. Don't buy me anything.'

This was the man who claimed to love me and want a baby with me. The man who had rung me nearly every day for the last seven months. Now he was telling me I was only good for one thing? And he didn't want the birthday present I'd bought for him?

Did I mean anything to him?

In that moment it was like I finally saw our relationship for what it was. I told him I didn't want to speak to him again.

He texted me later.

'I'd rather you return it and have money in the bank – save you doing another teeth whitening job. I'd rather you show me your love physically... I'd be much happier if you got a refund and spent it on nice things for the kids.'

And then he messaged me the next day accusing me of 'creeping' AKA cheating in his dream the previous night. He was toying with me again.

'You've told me you don't want this bracelet,' I replied, 'but you still expect me to be loyal to you? For what?'

'Sorry,' he wrote. 'I'm such a prick. I feel bad leaving on bad energy.'

'David, I loved you so much.'

'Where did you see us going from here?'

'Well, I'll be going mental.'

I was done with him. I wasn't going to put myself through it any longer.

He tried to win me round by sending me silly memes.

'Hope this one makes you smile?' he wrote.

'No, it doesn't,' was my blunt reply.

He sent me a picture of himself, declaring it 'a beautiful view'.

'A thing of nightmares, more like,' I wrote back.

He even WhatsApped me a photo of him and Sian on holiday skiing. Why would he do that?

'Sending good vibes from Verbier,' he wrote.

'Shame there wasn't an avalanche,' I replied.

On December 10th, the newspapers broke the story of our relationship. I'm amazed it had stayed under wraps for so long because so many people knew about us, but the Mirror had it on the front page and claimed I'd joined the throuple.

I started getting trolled on Instagram and TikTok. I was called a 'whore' and sent a whole heap of abuse which was tough to take. I'd worked hard for my career; I was a mum, I had to go and do the school run and my sex life was now a national conversation.

I'm not saying I'm a perfect innocent angel, and I know that I had plenty of opportunities to walk away, but my intentions for David were only ever pure.

I was in love with him, and breaking away wasn't going to be easy, but I knew I had to cut contact if I was to have any chance of finding peace and rebuilding my sense of self.

'I will feel strong again, but I need space,' I wrote. 'You trigger me. You said you loved me, but you don't. I feel like you lied to me the whole time about how you felt about me. I need to look after myself for my babies who need their mum.'

He messaged to say he hoped I had a good Christmas.

'I hope you have a shit Christmas, David,' was my reply.

I've never spoken to him since and he's blocked on my phone. But even though he was no longer in my life and I might have been physically free, shaking him out of my system has been a process and the whole relationship has had a profound, long-lasting effect on me. Finishing with him was a bit like escaping a burning building – I'd made it out alive, but the toxic smoke lingered in my lungs.

In fact, I'm as certain as I can be that meeting David was a contributory factor to the breakdown which was just around the corner and would threaten everything I held dear – my kids, my career and my health.

Those wheels were set in motion and I was now hurtling towards disaster. And there was nothing I could do about it.

Chapter Thirteen

The Unravelling

DECEMBER 2023 WOULD BE THE second Christmas that Scott and I had been separated and during a moment of weakness I'd agreed to him having the children over the holiday. It was on the condition that I could take them away with me to Bali for New Year, but I knew that being apart from Matilda, Delilah and Charlie on Christmas Day was going to be really tough for me.

I live and breathe my kids and it killed me to think that we wouldn't be dressing up in our matching Christmas pyjamas and putting food out for the reindeer. I wouldn't hear their excited squeals in the morning as they opened their stockings from Santa.

They went down to Scott's the day before Christmas Eve, and I tried to take my mind off how bereft I was by heading out to an event that night where I drank myself into oblivion. It was an attempt to drown my sorrows, but I ended up making things decidedly worse for myself.

Totally smashed, I followed a guy I vaguely knew on to a club but when he saw me there, he looked at me with total disdain and said, 'What are you doing?' and I realised that I must have appeared desperate.

Embarrassed. Humiliated. Rejected.

I didn't even know why I'd gone… I think I just wanted a hug. How sad is that? And how pathetic, thinking I was going to find comfort from some random bloke I barely knew.

I didn't want to go back to an empty house that night – it was too vast, still and quiet when the kids weren't there – so instead I got a taxi alone to my parents' and went to sleep, curled up in the foetal position in the bedroom I'd had as a little girl.

I felt so, so lonely.

When I woke up the next morning and looked at the clock on my phone, I remembered I had an appointment with the doctor about my PMDD in, like, 20 minutes' time. Shit.

I couldn't miss that appointment. My symptoms had recently reached unbearable levels of awfulness and I needed answers and support. I was still caked in last night's make-up, I had my lashes on and my hair extensions in, and I was wearing the same dress, but I called an Uber, zero fucks given, and arrived at the doctor's looking like I'd just done the walk of shame.

I think that was a sign of what a bad way I was in and the receptionist ushered me forward to see the doctor straightaway, probably realising that she had a live one here.

I spilled everything out to the GP; detailing how terrible things had got with my cycle, and that I didn't think I could cope with it anymore. His solution was to prescribe me with the Yasmin contraceptive pill because for some women it can help reduce hormonal fluctuations, ease water retention and bloating, as well as stabilising other symptoms.

I'd never taken the pill before and almost immediately it didn't agree with me. It made me feel very sick. I've since learned that my history of hyperemesis gravidarum made me more hormonally sensitive and therefore more pre-disposed to nausea when taking Yasmin.

And I know this might sound a bit OTT, but it also seemed to bring on a depression about my fertility burning away. I told myself to carry on because the doctor had assured me it was going to help me in the long run.

God, Christmas Day was dismal. I spent most of it in bed, missing my kids, stressed about my PMDD and devastated over David. I was a ticking time bomb of emotional chaos.

On top of all this, I'd recently signed a contract to star as Miss Scarlett in a touring theatre production of *Cluedo 2*, a camp comedy mystery inspired by the board game. Rehearsals were due to start in January and the show would play multiple dates across the country over several months in 2024.

I was excited to be getting back into acting after a long spell out of the industry, and the role of Miss Scarlett felt perfect for me, but as the start date drew nearer, a terrible anxiety about leaving the children for days at a time started to build. We would be six months on the road, and obviously I'd get back in between, but I was going to miss them so much.

I picked the kids up from Scott on Boxing Day – we always met halfway at Birmingham for handovers – and we flew to Bali on the 27th, a holiday which ended up being fraught with upset as I grappled with the mayhem in my head.

While we were there, poor Matilda developed Bell's Palsy, a paralysis of the face which had been brought on by an eye infection. It was a frightening experience for her, and me, and I felt like I couldn't cope with all this heaviness at once.

My life was like a pressure cooker and while in Bali, I called my doctor at The Priory to make sure I was going to have enough Concerta to get me through January.

Knowing my prescription was going to be ready for me to collect as soon as I landed back in the UK was a tiny crumb of comfort – at least that was one thing I could depend on.

* * *

It was the evening of January 8th, 2024 when the world as I knew it collapsed. Since returning from Bali and especially over the days before, I'd felt a loosening of my grip on reality, a growing sense of paranoia and an inability to stay on top of the daily routine.

I'd put it down to tiredness, depression and stress. But then came the voices in my head, the hallucinations and delusions and by that point it was too late to claw my way back.

That night, I became convinced there were men on my drive trying to break into the house with me and the kids inside – I called the police who came round very quickly and searched the area and told me it was clear.

I called them three times that night and on each visit they assured me no one was there, but I didn't – couldn't – believe them.

I opened all the windows upstairs.

'I can see you, you fucking bastards!' I yelled to the men prowling outside. 'Don't you dare come any closer!'

I went into the bedroom in a rage which started at my toes and moved all the way up my body until I was paralysed with this anger, lying horizontally at the bottom of the bed while Matilda, Delilah and Charlie slept soundly at the top – all of them liked to co-sleep with me. I found myself remembering incidents, conversations and experiences from the past which I'd long forgotten, like I was watching a movie of my life flashing before me.

I know now that I was in a psychosis, a highly disturbed mental state where you lose contact with what's real. Thoughts become distorted, disjointed and confused and the sufferer can become severely suspicious of other people or convinced of things which don't match up with reality.

I'd got it into my head that my neighbour across the back was trying to kill me, and I'd concocted this ludicrous story in my head that he was a drug smuggler, working with Scott. To me, this explained why Scott had always refused to have security cameras on the property.

I'd always hated having a safe in the house. I thought it put me and the kids at risk and I knew only too well the horror stories of footballers' houses being targeted by thieves – I still carried the trauma of the break-in we had ourselves in Prestbury more than 10 years before.

By morning I was exhausted because I hadn't slept a wink, but at least the daylight made me feel safe. No one was going to get me now.

I took a Concerta tablet from my bedroom drawer, which was going to help me focus on getting through the day, then I got the kids' uniforms ready and prepared us all breakfast. But I was disconnected, almost drifting through a parallel universe and while the children were eating, I became distracted and weirdly fascinated with my garden. I can't remember how long I spent just staring at it.

On some level, I was aware that I had a busy day ahead

filming some lingerie content in Manchester for Ann Summers. As usual, my friend Ashley was going to shoot this for me although I wasn't too sure how it would look because my face was an absolute mess; showing all the signs of someone who hadn't slept, with bags and black circles underneath my eyes and tired, grey skin. But I thought if we just whacked a load of concealer on, I'd get away with it.

By now I was ridiculously late for the school run, so I bundled the kids into the car, shaking as I did so and looking over my shoulder in case someone jumped out on us. I dropped off Matilda and Delilah first, and then drove on to Charlie's nursery.

I remember him telling me on the way that he needed a wee, but it's like it didn't register with me – I kept on driving and the poor little mite, who wasn't long out of nappies, wet himself in his car seat. I parked up outside the nursery, scooped him up and walked to his classroom and I'll never forget how the nursery teacher looked at me, like she just wanted to get Charlie off me as quickly as possible.

She was clearly concerned for his safety, and now I understand why because I must have been behaving like a total oddball and I know I looked a right state, wired through lack of sleep.

'He's wet,' she said, as she took him from my arms.

'Oh, really?' I replied, blasé.

I think she thought I was off my face on drugs.

I kissed Charlie goodbye, told him I loved him and drove to Manchester, ringing Scott on the way to tell him I wanted the safe out the house and security cameras installed because it was putting me and the kids in danger. He wasn't particularly sympathetic which got me even more angry – relations between us were pretty dire.

I had a room reserved in a hotel where Ashley was already waiting for me to shoot this Valentine's Day content. She grimaced at my knackered face and said she'd try her best, but as she was doing my make-up, I could see a man masturbating in the window.

He was right there, clear as day.

I shrieked.

'Ashley, look at that bloke! He's wanking himself off!'

But she couldn't see anything.

'Do you need your eyes tested, Helen?! There's no one there.'

'How can't you see him?'

'Oh my god, you're losing the plot!'

We both started laughing because it was such a daft situation and Ashley thought I was just messing about.

'Just Helen being Helen,' she assumed. 'Off on one again!' not twigging that I was in the middle of a psychotic episode. Which is a bit of a worry because my behaviour was top-level bonkers.

Regardless of the existence of the 'tosser' in the window, we carried on with the hair and make-up, but none of the content we shot that day got approved by

Ann Summers because I was on another planet and my face was a shambles. No amount of concealer was going to save me, the pictures simply weren't usable.

My nanny Regie was picking up the kids that day, so after we'd finished the shoot which was never to see the light of day, I took another Concerta to calm me down and walked into town. There were often paps hanging around Manchester city centre and I started to get paranoid about being photographed with my face looking the way it did, so I returned to the hotel to pick up my car and then drive back to Bolton.

I asked the staff on reception to check there were no paps outside and told them that I was scared someone was going to stab me. I said there were people out to get me and that I feared for my life.

This lovely guy who worked behind the desk seemed to clock that I wasn't well and said he'd personally walk me back to my car if I didn't feel safe. He also kindly offered to accompany me while I drove out of the car park, only I totally forgot he was in the car, and I started to drive away from the city centre and back to Bolton. I was oblivious.

'Um, can you let me out?' he said, a bit bemused. 'I need to get back to work.'

This poor guy! I had to turn around and take him back to Manchester.

I set off again, but then became distracted by something moving about in the boot. I could see it moving up and down and it actually makes me feel ill remembering this because my eyes were not on the road at all. It's a miracle I didn't crash the car – things could have turned out so differently, but somehow I got back to the house in one piece.

Regie was there with the kids, and I told her to stay inside while I checked the gardens for the men who were out to get us.

'What are you talking about, Helen?'

'Just get inside and keep the kids close.'

This was the middle of winter and it was dark, so I put the torch on my iPhone as I searched all around the grounds of the house, and once I was satisfied the coast was clear, I went into the kitchen and opened a bottle of wine.

I was stressed about the upcoming theatre tour and being away from the kids. I'd had the most horrible 24 hours with the supposed break-ins and the men who wanted me dead, and I needed alcohol to settle my nerves.

Regie told me to sit down and take some deep breaths.

'I don't know what's going on, but you need to calm down,' she said.

Then I looked out the window and I could 'see' my neighbour staring at me, the one Scott was smuggling the drugs with.

'Regie, can you see that guy? He's been spying on me because he's trying to kill me.'

She looked at me as if I was nuts.

'I'm telling you, he's plotting to do me in.'

'I can't see anyone staring. You're scaring me, Helen.'

I told her my theory about Scott and this neighbour being in cahoots together and how the drugs were locked in the safe. I was so agitated. I ran upstairs for a better vantage point and saw another man watching me from the park opposite. I began screaming at Regie.

'Helen,' she pleaded with me, 'there's no one there. Please, believe me.'

I was clutching the banister and started getting angry with Regie for not being able to see what I was seeing. At some point she must have phoned my parents because suddenly they arrived at the door and that made me even more furious.

'How fucking dare you call them! I'm only trying to protect my children!'

It sends a chill down my spine to think of how I spoke to Regie that night – she's a good friend who was only trying to help – but I wasn't myself and I couldn't think straight. And I'm so relieved now that it was my parents who came and not Scott because the psychosis had made me so certain he wanted me dead, I think there's a high chance I would have attacked him and tried to kill him first. I don't say any of this lightly – that's how much of a stranglehold this thing had on me.

My dad, who has always been a calming presence in my life, sat me down on the bed and spoke to me very gently.

'Helen, we think you've had a bad reaction to your medication. What's going to happen now is we're going to take the children back to our house.'

Apart from my pregnancies and during breastfeeding, I'd taken Concerta since the age of 16, but there was now so much of it in my system, I'd actually call it a form of drug abuse. There was no one keeping an eye on my prescription – I'd just get it renewed every few months, and I can see that by now I was addicted. I liked how they made me feel and I'd get very jittery if I'd gone too long between tablets.

In fact, there were occasions I'd take three in one go. I'd been told that I could take extra if I felt the need but when I'd taken too many, I'd get nosebleeds so it clearly wasn't doing me any good.

I told my dad that the red light on the TV was a camera and that was proof I was being watched by the neighbours, who were working for Scott. I said they were possibly even drugging me in my sleep and they were the ones who were making me crazy.

Matilda came into the bedroom crying and she sat down on my lap because she didn't want to leave me. I told her how much I loved her before my mum came in and led her away.

'You need to come with me and your mum as well,' said my dad.

No way. No chance.

All the complexities of my relationship with my mum

which had been festering since the first day I had a hormone in my body, came rushing to the fore.

'Absolutely fucking not,' I replied. 'You can take the kids, but I'm not going anywhere *she* is. I'd rather be here with robbers.'

My dad started to cry and he said I was reminding him of my brother and I later felt so embarrassed and guilty that my parents and kids had seen me like that. My lowest possible ebb.

Still sipping from this bottle of wine I wouldn't let go of, I continued to refuse to go back to my parents' although obviously I wasn't fit to be left alone. I finally agreed to go with Regie to the house she shared with her family and where she put me to bed in her room.

I became fixated on her patterned wallpaper which had ladies dancing and chandeliers and it made me feel like I was tripping. Then the red light of her TV seemed to come right up to my face and I started seeing mermaids and the devil in the form of a spider.

Eventually I drifted off to sleep.

* * *

When I woke up the next morning, I had a gazillion missed calls. I was supposed to be doing live radio interviews to promote *Cluedo 2* and the poor press lady from the show had been ringing to get me set up.

I barely knew where the hell I was. Or who I was.

I'm normally fine doing live interviews. It wouldn't

usually be a bother, but I was in no state. I called the publicist back and told her what had happened the night before – she said to take it easy and that she'd cancel the interviews.

Regie dropped me at my parents' house and I was pleased to see the kids, but had a big row with my mum because I was due over in Manchester for a voice coaching session for Miss Scarlett, who had an RP (received pronunciation) accent and she didn't think it was a good idea for me to go.

'You need to rest and sort yourself out,' she said, urging me to stay. 'Rearrange the voice coaching for another day, today is not a good day.'

I didn't respond well to this. I saw it as my mum trying to control me and I told her this was all her fault which was horrible of me. Ignoring her advice, I headed to Manchester looking hellish, eyes still bruised and my hair scraped up in a bun. I'm not even sure if I'd brushed my teeth.

I made the session but can't remember anything about it and this hapless voice coach must have thought I was a complete nutter. I rang up the director straight after and begged him not to sack me for having missed the media round that morning.

'Of course, I'm not going to sack you,' he said. 'It's too late notice now, anyway.'

I was very conflicted about carrying on with the tour, though. My parents were dead against me doing it because they recognised that I needed to stay home, find help and get well. But I'd signed my contract and to back out now would be letting a lot of people down, not to mention how unprofessional it would look.

Who would ever employ me again after that?

I was due in London in a few days' time for the first of three weeks of rehearsals, but knowing how much I'd been declining mentally, I wouldn't have been able to trust myself to stay in a hotel room on my own. I remember that feeling so powerfully. For a while I'd thought there was a real possibility that I might hurt myself.

Instead (and this literally makes me hold my head in my hands just thinking about it). I was planning to stay the three weeks with a model guy I'd met on Raya.

Wild, right? What a genius solution that was.

If I ever needed proof I was off my trolley, surely this was it.

We'd been on a date in early January and our night out at Soho House had ended with him telling me I was the weirdest girl he'd ever met. Undeterred, I'd invited him back to my hotel room, just to chill – I didn't want to sleep with him under any circumstances because causal sex is always guaranteed to make me feel rubbish the next day, but as soon as we stepped through the door of my room, he was like a ninja with his boxers off.

'Oh no!' I said, covering my eyes. 'You're a nice guy but I genuinely didn't mean that.'

To be fair, he was very respectful and we just had a

cuddle instead and that's when I'd asked if I could come and stay with him when I was down for rehearsals later in the month.

'Sure,' he said. 'It'll be fun.'

So that was where I was planning to base myself.

As I was packing my suitcase, getting ready to take the train down to London later that day for the first week of rehearsals, Matilda was crying which was heartbreaking for me.

'Daddy's gone and now you're going too,' she said. 'Don't you love me? I don't want to go to Grandma's house.'

She was only eight and she'd already been through me and Scott splitting up and him moving away. She'd witnessed much of my breakdown over the previous week and it was a lot for a little girl to take.

Too much.

Then this Raya guy texted and said he could now only accommodate me for three nights because he was going skiing with his friends. It was like a sign. I didn't want to fail or cause anyone a problem, and I really wanted to do this show, but I knew then I couldn't continue. I wasn't well enough to do it.

I called my agent Robin, told him everything and he instructed me to switch my phone off, promising that he would sort everything out. He then travelled up to see me at the house where he found me on the sofa, not really able to speak.

I'd stopped taking my Concerta, too scared of another

psychotic episode to go there again. But I'd still needed something, so I'd gone to the doctor, who had prescribed a different kind of medication for ADHD which I'd taken immediately, searching for a way out of this horrific slump. Anything that would help me escape the hell inside my head.

But it was like those new pills broke my brain. Robin was here, sitting on my sofa and I was unable to function. That's when together with my dad, he removed every single bit of medication out of the cupboards and out of the house and arranged for me to see a psychiatrist at The Priory.

Robin took care of the paperwork I needed for the theatre company's insurers, which confirmed that I wasn't mentally fit to go ahead with the production and I'm so grateful they didn't sue me because I was obviously in breach of my contract and had caused a major crisis just as rehearsals were due to start.

Luckily, they were able to get Ellie Leach to replace me, which was amazing because she was fresh off the back of winning *Strictly Come Dancing* and a fabulous name to have on the bill. She's Brooke Vincent's cousin, so we had a longstanding connection and I was so pleased it was her who was able to step in.

I agreed with Robin and my parents to come off social media for an extended period while I worked on my recovery – Instagram is my bread and butter but I needed to avoid any external noise and just focus on getting better. My friends weren't able to get hold of me for weeks because I also turned my phone off, too stressed and not strong enough to deal with anything other than the very minute I was living in.

The kids were at my mum and dad's and they stayed there for about a month. I saw them every day but I couldn't look after them on my own and that was a distressing reality to accept. Charlie's nursery was in regular contact and needed to know from a safeguarding perspective that the kids were being cared for primarily by my parents.

Much of that time is such a blur and I think I've blanked a lot of it out, a form of self-preservation, protecting myself from the emotional pain associated with those memories.

I was off all forms of medication and spent my days looking after the children with my mum and dad in between sessions at The Priory.

I was very rarely alone. My dad stayed with me regularly as did my friend Jay and my agent Robin was around a lot, too

Scott also came to stay for a few days which was strange because this was mid-season and he was supposed to be in training with Bristol Rovers. I don't know if my parents had been in touch and told him he needed to come up to support me and the children, but it didn't occur to me to ask questions, I was just glad he was here.

I was craving familiarity and he was actually really nice

to me in the days he stayed, I think he was shocked by how unwell I'd become.

It did briefly cross my mind that we might get back together… perhaps this would give us the kick to give things another go. But that was my vulnerability talking and I know it would never have worked.

I know at some point I rang up the nursery teacher because I was worried that they might notify social services and the kids would be taken off me. I needed the staff to know that I didn't take drugs and even went down there in person to show them my medical notes which explained that the psychosis had been a reaction to my medication.

The teacher told me that her priority was always Charlie and his health and wellbeing and that she hoped I got myself better. Delilah had gone to that nursery too, so they knew I was a good mum and all this was out of character, but obviously safeguarding comes first and foremost, so they stayed across the situation and were in constant touch with my parents.

I felt like I had nothing. I thought I must surely be the shittest mum ever and was certain that I'd ruined my career and would never work again. I'd flushed it all down the toilet.

I was losing all my money, losing my kids. My finances were atrocious and I couldn't see how anything was ever going to get better. Everyone was keeping tabs on me and trying to control me.

HEAD & HEART

I couldn't stop crying about the children, about Scott, about David.

Everything I'd worked hard for was being taken away from me and I struggled to see a way back from how low I'd sunk.

Chapter Fourteen

Recovery

MAYBE THE BREAKDOWN WAS A blessing in disguise because it forced me to stop.

In the run-up to everything crashing down, I had fallen into such a deeply depressive mindset that something needed to give. I can see that now.

If I'd tried to push through it, ignoring the advice of everyone around me and gone down to London in the state I was in, then I honestly believe something awful would have happened. I don't want to think about that for too long because it gives me the shivers.

For the next three months, I checked out of the public eye, switched off all my social media and focused on getting well. The period of psychosis, although scary and very difficult for me to revisit, even now as I write about it, turned out to be my saving grace.

I was medication-free, having regular therapy and little

by little I started to feel mentally stronger. By the middle of February, the children were back with me, which was amazing, although Mum and Dad were still heavily involved and visited daily for long periods.

I deliberately kept a low profile during this time and avoided going anywhere I was likely to be papped. I certainly didn't need the complications that come with being in the media.

Admittedly though, by the end of February I was climbing the walls for a night out. I'd been confined to the house for the best part of two months; I was being constantly watched by my parents and it all felt so claustrophobic. I couldn't bear it.

I wasn't allowed to work and because I'd come off my socials, I had no outlet. I wanted to escape for a little while and taste a bit of life again, if only for a few hours.

My friend Jodie suggested we go for a couple of quiet drinks in Alderley Edge and I jumped at the chance, although my mum and dad were strongly opposed to the idea because they wouldn't be able to monitor my every move.

I put on some make-up and did my hair and wore a mini skirt with black thigh-high boots which was a million miles away from the slobby joggers style I'd been decked out in for the last few weeks. I felt more like my old self again, almost normal.

So, there we were in this bar enjoying a couple of Proseccos and it was nice being out with Jodie, who has been one of my best and most fabulous mates for more than 10 years. We gravitated in the direction of a nice gay couple we'd spotted across the bar and who looked like they'd be fun to chat to – I generally have good gaydar, and their bright white teeth, immaculate grooming and healthy-looking tans were dead giveaways to me. But as soon as Robbie Talbot and his mate Richie opened their mouths, I knew they were straight.

The four of us hit it off. Robbie was funny and charming and told me he'd not long split from his fiancée and was staying at Richie's place while he sorted himself out with somewhere permanent to live.

We all ended up quite tipsy and me and Robbie were getting flirtatious although a protective Jodie put a stop to all that by calling time on the night and taking me home. But not before I'd given Robbie my number.

We started texting the next day and after about a week of messaging, he asked if I fancied going out to dinner sometime. I was quite keen to see him again, so tentatively accepted and we had a nice date the following week at Victors in Hale – a deliberately low-key choice of venue and not somewhere I was going to get pictured.

I wasn't too sure it was going to go anywhere and I definitely didn't want anything serious, but Robbie made me laugh and he had a lovely gentlemanly, almost old-fashioned way about him which I liked a lot.

He was also very generous with his time, a really dependable kind of guy and would go out of his way to help anyone who needed it. A case in point: I went down to Birmingham to see my friend Jay and had my phone stolen by a security guard at a big clothing store. It turned out to be part of a big organised crime operation – this guy would rob the phones in the shop and then pass them on to someone else to clean up and resell.

When I realised my phone had been nicked, I tracked it on the iPad and discovered that it was at a residential address in Birmingham – all my pictures were on there, and (typical me) nothing was backed up, so it was vital that I got it back.

By now I was at home in Bolton, but I decided I was going to drive down to Birmingham the next day, knock on the door and offer a few hundred quid in exchange for the phone. For obvious reasons, I didn't want to risk doing it alone, so I rang Robbie and straightaway he offered to come with me.

We got to the house and the people who answered the door were dodgy as fuck, so I was extremely grateful to have Robbie there as back-up and with a bit of negotiation plus a wodge of cash, we managed to get the phone returned.

I kind of felt with Robbie that if I'd said I needed to go to the Outer Hebrides tomorrow, he would have dropped everything to accompany me. He was caring and kind and he made me feel safe.

At the end of March, he drove me all the way down to Brighton to watch *Cluedo 2* at the Theatre Royal – despite everything that had happened I really wanted to go see the show. I knew it was going to be hard for me to watch because in another world it would have been me up on the stage, but having Robbie there made the experience easier.

He made a special evening of it by taking me for a nice dinner beforehand and he held and squeezed my hand throughout the performance. He was just so sweet and sensitive the way he handled everything.

We started dating properly after that, but I didn't sleep with him for quite a while. I made him wait as I felt quite fragile about sex and wanted to be sure we weren't just a flash in the pan before I went to bed with him.

Once we crossed that line, things intensified between us and we were both now serious about each other. He was a good-looking guy with a lot of charisma, affectionate, patient and gentle with me, and I loved the cheeky Scouse persona.

I also liked that he was older and that he understood my kids were always going to be my priority. I saw what a good dad he was to his own children, although I held off introducing him to Matilda, Delilah and Charlie until the summer.

Matilda, understandably, dished him out a lot of attitude and sass at the start, but Robbie just took it in his stride and gave her space. With a bit of time, she started to come round and he was brilliant with the kids. He was so silly with them, telling them stories which the girls were obsessed with; he'd play football in the garden with them, and he was a big help to me both in the house and when getting out and about.

I felt good with Robbie and I knew he wasn't going to hurt me, mess me about or play mind games. He treated me well, bringing a bit of calm and stability to my life and he was supportive of everything I did, even when I told him I was contracted to do *Celebs Go Dating* with E4, a show I'd signed up for before we were an item.

I'd had months without any income and, with a looming tax bill, I couldn't afford not to work anymore. I'd already had to sell off loads of my handbags just to try and keep my head above water.

I explained to Robbie that *Celebs Go Dating* was just a job and it wouldn't affect how I felt about him – I'd go down to London, do what I needed to do to make a TV show and that would be it.

He was totally understanding.

'No problem,' he said. 'You go and get your dough, girl.'

He knew all about the show and that it would see me 'dating' other men, but he went along with it, even picking me up from the station after I'd been filming down south.

The boys on *Celebs Go Dating* were all gorgeous, but I was so into Robbie that I wasn't tempted and my head wasn't turned at all. Nevertheless, I knew that I had a role to play there – part of the job I was hired to do was to make good telly, so when I snogged Luke on one of the dates, I looked at it as filming a scene. This is what I'd done from the age of nine, so it was second nature to me.

Luke was fit so it wasn't that hard! But he was also 10 years younger than me, so even if I'd been single, it was never going to be anything serious, and when I broke things off, I was being honest, saying I didn't see a future with him.

Although, obviously, it wasn't only the age gap putting me off.

When the news came out during filming that I had a 'secret' boyfriend in real life and I was confronted by the agents, I was forced to fess up in front of the cameras.

Awks.

The revelation brought proceedings to a halt mid-series and Paul, Anna and Dr Tara looked so disappointed in me, like I was a naughty schoolgirl who had personally let them down! I held my hands up and admitted that yes, there was someone in my life, who I had strong feelings for.

The agents might have been annoyed with me, but as far as the producers were concerned, it was a dynamite storyline and they got a ton of press from this twist in the tale so I can't say I was overridden with guilt. I'd also been honest about Robbie off camera with the guys I'd dated so I wasn't duping anybody and nobody got hurt.

Producers were keen to get Robbie on the show so they could document our journey as a couple and put us through some therapy sessions with the agents. He was reluctant at first, but when he saw that it was going to get me out of a bit of a hole, he eventually agreed to it and came down to London to film scenes with Paul and Dr Tara.

Although this whole media malarkey wasn't his 'world' at all, he found it a laugh in the end and I guess that was a very public first declaration of our relationship.

But while that side of things turned out rather well, there were other aspects of *Celebs Go Dating* which were much more problematic for me. During the one-to-one sessions on the coaching couch, I'd disclosed a lot about my affair with David Haye the previous year and that reopened wounds that had barely healed.

It was too soon and I had to book a series of sessions with my therapist straight after filming because talking about it like that proved hugely distressing.

I'd also completely overshared on camera about some of the confusion I was feeling around my sexuality. I think it can be quite natural and normal to experience this, especially when you're going through puberty and your teens. When I was 16, I remember confiding in my brother, who is very similar to me in personality, that I thought I liked girls too. He was kind with me.

I told him that I had a crush on one of my female friends, but couldn't work out if I really loved her or just wanted to be her.

I could never have told my mother any of this as she absolutely would not have accepted it – around this time she'd found out that I'd kissed a girl on a night out and her response was to tell me I needed therapy. After that I suppressed any feelings and maybe even felt some shame around them.

I'm definitely sexually attracted to men, but during my 13-year relationship, sexuality was something that I thought about privately and often wished that I'd explored it more when I was younger and had the chance. Perhaps I could have got to know myself a bit better.

When Scott and I finished, it gave me the space to have a real look at myself and who I was. Sadly for me (!) I came to the conclusion that I do indeed still like men, but I think experimentation can be a healthy thing to do if you're in a bit of a muddle about how you feel or who you are.

However, once I'd poured my heart out about it to the agents on *Celebs Go Dating*, I knew this 'confession' would be picked up by the papers and I started to panic about the impact it would have on my family and specifically my mum.

I honestly don't care if anyone is gay, lesbian, bi, whatever, it's not important to me. But it would be to my mum who, despite our differences, I love and respect. I'm nothing like her – she wears Laura Ashley and goes to craft club for starters – but that doesn't mean I don't value having her as part of my life and my children's lives.

I've always wanted to be close to my mum and to make her proud and I was sure I'd appalled her enough times over the years already; the thought of this footage going out on national telly got me really depressed, like I'd massively let her down as a daughter.

I also thought I was going to be hated by other women for admitting sleeping with David when he had a girlfriend and I got in a proper spiral with my OCD and anxiety about the edit and how it was going to come across.

The OCD was crushing me with the darkest of thoughts, some of which spun off into the suicidal. I'd wake up in the morning, wet through from the sweats and feeling sick. I had to be around people all the time because I knew I wasn't safe to be on my own.

Thankfully, the producers at the show were understanding and they agreed to edit those scenes alongside me, something they did with great care, removing the parts completely where I opened up about my sexuality.

The producer said, 'Maybe you can write all that in a book one day...'

And, well, here we are.

* * *

Robbie didn't ever move in with me, but in September 2024 I did ask him to stay for a while because my house is so big and I feel safer if there's another adult there. I get scared on my own.

It was hard work at first because I still co-slept with all three kids, so I had to get them into their own beds. I was trying my best with everything; to be a good mum, to keep my head together, to work and to stay financially afloat. I don't think I was doing a particularly amazing job at any of those things, but I also know I need to cut myself a bit of slack now and then, something I've never been very good at.

I thought I'd be happy with Robbie. He's Northern, down to earth and very loving and I knew he loved me. But having him in the house soon felt kind of jumbled. I didn't want to be making his tea every evening or cleaning his skids off the toilet! I'd done all that before.

Him being there all the time also made me start to miss Scott. Like, badly.

Even though Robbie was always dead nice, having him around the kids so much started to trigger me and I'd get flashbacks of when me, Scott and the children had lived in this house together.

It just got too much.

There were other issues too, which became much more obvious now that we were spending all our time together. Alcohol could be an issue for us. I don't think I ever spent a day with him when he wasn't drinking.

He's a good drunk, there was no badness in him, but it was getting quite difficult to watch, because, in my eyes, he was slowly killing himself. We went to Dublin for his birthday weekend and I can't even tell you how much Guinness he drank in that time, but I had no idea how he was still standing.

I knew Robbie came from a tough background and he hadn't had the easiest of starts in life.

I thought I'd be able to help him and tried to suggest he had sparkling water rather than Guinness. I encouraged him to get fit and go for a run to help develop a healthier mindset.

There were financial difficulties as well, way too complex for me to take on. Robbie had lost his business during Covid and things were tough.

When he'd 'moved in' to my place, he'd turned up to my house with all his clothes in bin bags and that's when it struck me that my boyfriend was actually homeless.

There was a day when Scott came to pick up the kids, pulling into the driveway in his white G Wagon and getting out looking pristine, head-to-toe in Dior, while Robbie was in the house and dressed in his In The Style Christmas pyjamas. That was quite the moment for me.

I was torn because I knew if I sent him back to his mate's house, he wouldn't have my support. If he stayed with me, I could at least try and help him. But then that felt like a big responsibility and if I was being honest, I probably shouldn't have been in a relationship at all, let alone one which was such a can of worms. I needed to be looking after myself.

I was truthful with Robbie about how I felt – this was all happening too fast and although I didn't want to finish with him, I wanted my own space back, for the kids' sakes as well.

He took it well and said he'd known his moving in was only ever meant to be a temporary arrangement. He didn't see this as the end of us either – far from it. He loved me and was excited about what the future held for us.

We ended up having a really nice Christmas together and spent Christmas Eve in this tiny pub in Liverpool with all Robbie's friends, having the best night. That was something I'd never been able to do with Scott – professional footballers don't tend to drink in cosy locals because that would draw too much attention and risk attracting trouble. Footballers drink in exclusive venues with VIP areas and security and I really enjoyed being in the warmer, more comfortable setting of the pub.

I do feel that Robbie came along for a reason – having been so poorly in January and coming off the back of David, he was what I needed at that time and for a while at least, I did love him. But then he did something inexcusable which showed me another side to him.

It threw me under the bus and try as I might, I couldn't find it in myself to forgive him.

Chapter Fifteen

Court Out

THERE'S A TIKTOK TREND I'D love to do where you post a picture of yourself looking wistful and caption it, 'Me thinking I want a boyfriend…'

Then you stitch it to a second picture captioned, 'Me when I get a boyfriend…' and for that image my plan is to use the pap shot of me walking into Wirral Magistrates' court.

Welcome to my reality.

Since Robbie had lost everything with his business going under, he didn't have his own car and it was costing him a fortune to get about in Ubers. I felt sorry for him, and so in the summer of 2024, I arranged to have him insured on my Audi, telling him he could borrow it for a while as long as he was really careful with it.

Guys, he wasn't careful.

In the space of a fortnight, he managed to clock up three

speeding tickets – two in Liverpool and one in Manchester – so he was obviously bombing the car around like an idiot and without a care in the world.

When the letter from the police about the fines came through, because of the dates (and the fact I drive like a granny), I knew instantly it must have been Robbie who had been behind the wheel and I hit the roof.

'What were you playing at?' I asked him and all he could say was that he was sorry and he'd pay whatever was owed. Damned right he would!

There was a load of forms which had to be filled out within 28 days of receiving the letter – a Section 172 notice identifying the driver who can then be issued with a fixed penalty notice, usually a fine and points on their licence.

'You can sort this shit out,' I told Robbie. 'Your mess, you clear it up.'

Because of my ADHD, I've never been the best with admin or keeping on top of paperwork, but Robbie promised me he would sort it all out and accept the points. The only thing was, he didn't complete the documents correctly and on top of that, I hadn't realised that since the vehicle was registered to me, the forms were my responsibility regardless of who was driving.

And that's what landed me in court.

I hadn't got a Scooby about the amount of trouble I was in when I went along to the hearing in December 2024, confident that this was just a misunderstanding which would be easily resolved once I explained that I'd been confused over the paperwork.

But when I stood before the three magistrates that day and they started talking to me in lots of legal jargon which made no sense to me, I was flummoxed. I couldn't answer any of their queries and must have looked totally bewildered because in the end, the head magistrate told me to speak to a solicitor and then come back in January. He added that I should be aware that this was very serious and I was therefore facing a driving ban.

A ban?! I hadn't even been driving!

As we left the court, I whacked Robbie with my handbag.

'I can't get a ban! It was you who was speeding!'

The new court date wasn't until January 15th, so I tried mentally to brush it under the rug until then, but I hired a solicitor who helped me put together a case citing exceptional hardship to try and avoid a ban.

He told me I would have to explain to the court that I was a single mother of three, I had the kids with me 90 percent of the time and relied on the car to get them to and from school and all their various clubs. I also needed a car to attend my regular therapy sessions in Birmingham, which were key to maintaining my mental health.

It was important to emphasise to the magistrates that we lived in a rural village and that I wasn't in a financial position to pay for a driver or rely on taxis to run us about – I know everyone presumes that because my ex is a footballer and I've been on TV that I must be rolling in it, but that's not the case. While I'm not pleading poverty, neither am I cash rich and my solicitor told me I needed to make this very clear to the court.

What he didn't spell out to me was that these private details about my personal circumstances could and indeed *would* be made public under the principle of open justice. If I'd known that, I might have done things differently… At the very least I could have prepared myself for what was to come.

On the morning of the hearing, I had my hair blow-dried, my make-up done and I dressed all in black so I would look well presented in court. I was already nervous as me and Robbie walked towards the entrance, but I soon felt twice as bad when I saw a load of paps outside and the camera bulbs started flashing.

Inside the courtroom, there were about 10 journalists sitting in the gallery and I couldn't believe it. I knew the press had every right to be there, but I was shocked that this case – a minor driving offence – had attracted this much attention.

Did they know something I didn't? Did they think there was a possibility I was going to jail? OMFG, I wouldn't do well in prison. I wouldn't last a day.

I wanted to get it over with as quickly as possible. I was scared and intimidated because this was all new to me. I'd never been up in court for anything before.

I think the head magistrate could tell that I was a nice

girl who had landed in a pickle thanks to some poor judgement and the stupid behaviour of her boyfriend, but despite the case I'd prepared outlining the hardship losing my licence would cause, they issued me with six penalty points for each count of failing to give information relating to the identification of a driver, banned me for six months and fined me two grand.

So it had all been for nothing anyway.

There was such a lot of media present; I wanted to get as far away from the court as possible, so Robbie took me for a drink to steady my nerves. While we were sitting in the pub, stories about me being 'broke', along with details about my mental health taken from my statements to the court started to land online.

It was so upsetting, and I was mad all over again with Robbie that he'd put me in this position – not only was I without a driving licence, but I was also having to deal with excruciating elements of my private life being published across the internet.

I told him to book me an Uber so I could get home and back to my babies and he said he couldn't because he had no money until he got paid the following week.

That just about summed everything up in a nutshell.

I booked the taxi myself and I really should have just left Robbie there, but I took pity on him because it was snowing and he didn't have a coat. When we got back to mine, my nanny Regie who has always had my back, had a face like thunder. She was raging with Robbie.

'You've just lost Helen her licence!' she stormed. 'I can't believe you've done that to her and the kids, do you know how hard it's gonna be?'

There was nothing Robbie could do; he just stood there looking awkward and embarrassed, taking the full force of her fury.

If I'd thought the online coverage was bad, I'd seen nothing yet. I woke the next morning to articles right across the tabloid press, raking over every bit of the case I'd presented to the court and especially my finances. One paper had even published a photo of my house both online and in print which clearly put me and my kids at risk – when I take Instagram pictures, I'm always so careful about not showing any identifying details of our home.

The headlines were never-ending; I had journalists writing whole features about where my 'fortune' had gone and fake news articles littered with inaccuracies about how I was being 'forced' to sell the family home to sort out my 'financial woes'.

The truth about that was the night before the court case, I'd received a phone call from Scott to tell me that he needed to sell the house. It's an eight-bedroom property which is in his name and costs a fortune to run and it didn't make financial sense to hold on to it – he offered to keep it if I could take over the astronomical bills, but I wasn't in a position to do that.

Scott wasn't going to make us homeless – he would

never do that – and he promised to buy us somewhere else to live, but he couldn't afford to carry on forking out for the heating, electricity and water.

So, when he put the house on the market, it was nothing to do with my own money situation, but the media made it out that I was having to sell up to save myself from financial ruin. It was so humiliating thinking people were discussing my income and how 'strapped for cash' I was, having to do the school run with everyone thinking they knew the ins and outs of my earnings.

I actually do all right money-wise, but I do have to work. Scott doesn't 'fund' me, and yes, I had to adapt to living a much more frugal lifestyle when we split up – there are no more 20 grand holidays to Barbados which is what we used to do as the norm.

But that was fine by me. I'm proud that I've always worked, paid my dues and don't owe the tax man a penny. I'm a 'by the book' kind of person and even when times have been tight, I've always settled what I owe and have never dissolved a company just to write off debts.

With all this swirling around, no one could understand why I was still with Robbie. My mum already despised him (mainly because he wasn't Scott) and all of this just added to her hatred.

I think I was lying to myself about the relationship. I knew deep down it was over – it *had* to be over – but I wasn't ready to let go completely. Robbie had been there for me as I'd got back on my feet a year before; he'd been my anchor when I was sinking, and those emotional ties were strong.

But there were other cracks in the relationship besides the court case and his excessive drinking. For my Christmas present he'd arranged a weekend away at Grantley Hall in North Yorkshire, which he knew was somewhere Scott and I had used to go together. It had even been on my shortlist as a wedding venue.

It felt like a strange choice of gift, but it was booked for a couple of weeks after the court case when I really needed a break. I was definitely checking out of the relationship – there was a new ick unlocked every day – but I thought I'd go along to Grantley Hall and maybe I could pretend Robbie wasn't there while I enjoyed the spa.

When we were there, all I could think about was me and Scott and how much I'd hoped that one day we'd get married, and that was hard. Robbie was always very sweet with me, but there was something missing and I couldn't get over the part he'd played in putting me through that court case and its aftermath.

Scott suddenly seemed to loom large whatever I did. Robbie and I also spent a weekend in Glasgow where I'd felt Scott's presence constantly. We'd gone to the West End and I remembered how happy I'd been there when Scott was playing for Celtic and how different my life was now compared to back then. I had to go and have a little cry in some random pub toilets because it had reignited a lot of old feelings.

I started to distance myself from Robbie after that. We had some nice times together in February and March, but my heart wasn't in it anymore and Scott was playing on my mind so much which wasn't fair on anyone.

A few weeks after getting the driving ban, I'd gone to meet Scott for a drink at the Lowry in Manchester to discuss the sale of the house. We got on better than we had done in a long time – we even managed to have a bit of a laugh – and I had to admit to myself that I wasn't fully over him.

One night he FaceTimed me at about 2am when me and Robbie were asleep in bed. Scott is the father of my kids so I'm never going to ignore a phone call from him, but when I answered, he was just staring down the camera at me as if he was drunk – and Scott's never been a drinker.

I instantly recognised that he mustn't be in a good way, so I walked out of the bedroom and asked him if he was OK. I knew he was worried about football and money pressures, and also that he was unhappy about us – everything was messed up.

'Scott, I love you. Everything is going to be all right,' I tried to reassure him.

I told him I was going to put the phone down and we could talk in the morning, but even after I'd hung up, he kept on ringing. By now Robbie was awake and he was fuming.

'You still love your ex!' he shouted.

'I've told you how it is with me and Scott. He's always going to be in my life because of the children. And because of the children, I'll always love him. But I have never and would never cheat on you.'

It exploded into this massive argument and Robbie went and slept on the sofa while I got back into bed, my head spinning. It was a horrible situation to be stuck in the middle of, but that row had cleared a few things up for me, namely that I still had unresolved feelings for Scott and didn't have strong enough feelings for Robbie.

I couldn't see a future together, so there was little point in stringing this out although I knew I was going to break his heart.

A few days later, I told Robbie that hurting him was the last thing I ever wanted and that he was the nicest, kindest man I'd ever been with. I'd never had someone be so lovely with me before; he had made me happy and I still cared about him.

All true.

'But we're not right anymore, Robbie,' I continued. 'I've got loads going on and you have issues to deal with, too. I feel like I need to be on my own.'

I assured him that I wasn't splitting up with him to get back together with Scott or to start seeing anyone else for that matter. I said I'd meant it when I'd told him I loved him.

Robbie took it badly; I can't put it any other way.

He said he couldn't believe I was doing this to him

when everything else in his life was so difficult... but I can't take that on. I've got enough to worry about with my kids without carrying other people's problems and pain.

I've seen Robbie just once since that day, but he isn't part of my life anymore and I'm not sure we can be friends. Not yet, anyway.

Although I probably knew all along that he wasn't going to be my forever person, he did play an important role in my recovery and I'll always be grateful to him for that.

I wish him nothing but love and happiness.

I hope he finds it.

Chapter Sixteen

Facing the Future

I'M STARTING TO ENJOY BEING single. I'm getting used to it, anyway because I don't think now is the right time for me to be in a relationship. I've struggled with being alone in the past mainly because I don't particularly like my own company – believe me, this is something I'm working on.

In the past I think I've been guilty of using men as a bit of escapism. It's like I've always got to have someone 'there' who I'm either messaging or dating and it's possibly related to my ADHD and the dopamine dysregulation associated with the condition.

ADHD brains tend to have lower levels of dopamine or impaired dopamine signalling and that means we'll compensate by seeking out the 'hit' from other sources. It's not necessarily conscious, but it is a well-recognised behavioural pattern connected to neurodiversity.

I'll just come out and say it: I like male attention. It makes me feel better about myself; it makes me feel happier and I like the power it gives me. On the flip side of that, I suffer *terrible* rejection sensitivity. I had a one-night stand with a guy and then cried my eyes out all weekend because it was obviously just a bit of fun for him and wasn't going anywhere.

I'm all for sexually empowering women and I don't think we should be ashamed to say that, as females, we enjoy sex too. But although I'm a sexual person, I'm no good at having casual sex because when I've slept with someone, I feel connected to that person, so it really messes my head up if it turns out not to have meant as much to them.

And I know placing so much of my self-worth in what men think of me is a sign of something that's missing within. If I'm not noticed or wanted, if I don't get their approval, if they don't find me desirable, then I start to question myself and it makes me sad to acknowledge that. It's something I'm dealing with in therapy, hopefully to stop the damaging cycles and repeated behaviours which aren't serving me.

I need to be more aware of what I'm doing and why I'm doing it in order to look after myself and protect my heart better.

One of the issues has been trying to figure out the modern dating world which I re-entered almost completely blind after me and Scott split. I was totally inexperienced and quite innocent about the way a lot of men operate which is undoubtedly why I ended up with someone like David Haye.

I've since had my eyes opened to how players behave and the strategies they use, like breadcrumbing – a form of emotional manipulation where someone gives another person *just* enough attention to keep them hooked but with no intention of commitment – and I'm confident that I'll never get myself in a situation like I did with David again.

I know that it was bad for my mental health.

I don't want to come across as all 'woe is me' but it is so much harder to meet guys when you're in the public eye. That bloody Raya app has become way too incestuous – everyone on there has already shagged everyone else! I'm not even joking. It's like a bubble and you end up speaking to the same footballers, reality stars and models like a merry-go-round of sloppy seconds. Depressing as hell.

I got so fed up with Raya recently that I downloaded Hinge because all my non-famous friends on there seemed to be having a whale of a time. 'Fuck it,' I thought. 'Let's widen this dating pool.'

I set up my profile and within five minutes of putting it live, I started getting messages saying, 'Are you actually Helen Flanagan? What are you doing on Hinge?' Men were sending me 'roses' via the app and it all made me feel quite anxious – I worried about screenshots ending up in the press, something I really could have done without.

Then I saw one guy who caught my eye because he was super hot, but I quickly realised he was a footballer, FFS. I can't get away from them, not even there!

I've thought about taking some time out from dating. Maybe I should swear off men for a while, make myself the priority and learn to define myself on my own terms rather than through the male gaze.

I don't think I could ever take a vow of celibacy, though. By deliberately depriving myself of sex, I'd just end up thinking about it all the time and that would send me bloody loopy. It's a natural thing for humans to want to have a connection and to find that through sex. It's biologically hardwired into us.

What I *can* do is make a positive decision not to settle for the breadcrumbs and to accept that because I'm so sensitive when it comes to sex, I need to wait until I know someone properly before sleeping with them. I want to take a bit of a step back and make sure I'm more in tune with myself and what my triggers are.

I'm a hopeless romantic and I wouldn't want to change that about myself – I have a big heart, it's wide open and full of hope and I'm a firm believer in living life to the max. That openness means I feel things intensely and because of that I'm sometimes more liable to get hurt, but I'd rather risk that than go through life without feeling anything real.

Having said that, I don't think that I want to give another man my everything and I can't see myself getting married now. I think I'm a long way off settling down with anyone, not while I'm still attracted to men that are a little bit toxic.

Hopefully, by the time I reach my 40s, I'll have a more peaceful, contented life. And that's when I'll meet someone who loves me for me, who isn't going to screw me over and leave me heartbroken.

I still love romance and hope to have lots more of it, but what's more important to me these days is being independently and financially secure, so I plan to throw myself into my work and devote as much time as possible to my children.

I don't know where I'd be without the kids. They have saved me in so many ways, because no matter what has been going on in my life, as long as they're OK, I've been able to keep going and feel unconditional love.

Even on the darkest days.

Matilda is the most perfect little angel and has been since the day she was born. She gave me my purpose although we are different and our relationship can be a little bit like Eddie and Saffie in *Absolutely Fabulous*! I think having me as a mum means she's going to turn out the exact opposite i.e. super sensible. I feel like me and Matilda have grown up together – she's the sweetest soul, a little bit quirky and likes everything to be calm, very chilled like her dad and I'm proud of how I've always supported her having a strong relationship with Scott. She's absolutely divine in every way.

I'm obsessed with Delilah. I feel like she can talk to me about anything – she knows that I'm her safe place and that I've always got her back. Although she's close to a lot of people in her life, she's happiest when in my arms. She's a total free spirit and she's a brilliant little footballer.

And Charlie? Where do I start with my handsome prince? Charlie was a dream as a baby, but he is wild as a little boy! He runs around all day, jumps about, kicks everything and has a limitless supply of energy. I do tear my hair out with Charlie because I sometimes don't know what to do with him, but he's so funny and gorgeous I wouldn't have him any other way.

'Mummy,' he says, 'you are my queen.'

Being a mum is the hardest job in the world but it's also the best. None of us get it right 100 percent of the time and that's what I've learned over the years – sometimes I'm going to get it wrong and that's OK. All of us can only try our best.

Which brings me to Scott. I can't 'unlove' the father of my children and what I'm about to write is causing me great pain.

Whenever I've spoken publicly about Scott in interviews, I've always been generous to him. We have three children together and, at one time, he was the love of my life and so I will go out of my way to protect him.

But recently it's got to the point where I'm at the end

of my tether. The truth is, his decision to sell the family home where me and the children live has broken my heart. I remember so clearly the day he surprised me with the house and all the hopes I had for us in it. I poured all my savings into making it beautiful and it really has been my haven.

Scott isn't currently signed to a football club, so his reason for selling is purely financial and although I have tried to be understanding and compassionate about his situation, it makes me angry when he spends money on fancy holidays all summer as well as constant trips to Dubai.

Scott has other properties he could sell – his mother lives in a house which is similar to mine and yet that hasn't been put up for sale.

It would make me laugh if it wasn't so sad.

Watching people coming to view my house has been degrading, humiliating and extremely upsetting.

Although Scott covers the household bills, since he's been without a club, he has left me in a difficult position. I look after my children 90% of the time with the support of my amazing parents – just recently I've been making amends with my mum after a tricky few years and this has healed my heart. I love her very much.

But it's a juggle working full-time while bringing up three young children. If my mum and dad can't step in, I have to pay for a nanny. I've just signed up to do a reality show, which means I'll be away from the kids, but it's work. I have no choice.

I worry about the future and my security because it's impossible for me to save when everything I earn is needed here and now.

I know Scott loves his children deeply, but I need him to be a much more present father, not dipping in and out whenever he feels like it or seeing them once every fortnight.

I have to put my foot down with his constant demands that I meet him in Birmingham for handovers – that's a big journey for me there and back when I have work commitments. It was his decision to move to Bath, so he should be doing the bulk of the travelling.

Even though he has massively let me down, I will always love Scott and I've cried while writing this. He was all I ever wanted. But I am a woman with a voice and I would want my daughters to use theirs too if they were ever in the same position.

I think the moment I lost the plot with all this came in September when, looking for new ways to boost my income, I agreed to a meeting with the owners of OnlyFans about their new platform Subs.com.

I knew about Subs from my friend Christine McGuinness – she'd joined a few months before and she'd encouraged me to listen to what they had to say.

I love Christine, I think she's a fabulous person and an amazing mum who is doing her absolute best and I'd never belittle any woman who signs to OnlyFans. I understand we all do things for different reasons and I fully respect that, but this was never a route I wanted to go down myself. However, I was in a pretty precarious financial position and so thought I might as well hear them out.

I was in my PMDD week so not in the best frame of mind, but nothing about that meeting felt right. They told me I didn't have to do anything I didn't want to; it would just be lingerie pictures and all quite tame, but I couldn't shake the association with the OnlyFans brand or the knowledge that I'd have men paying to pervy message me.

It felt too grim. I didn't want that for myself. And I know I post underwear pictures on my social media all the time, but that's when I'm working for a lingerie or bikini brand. I'm not asking random creepy men to pay me for it.

One of the guys in the meeting was the most soulless man I'd ever met in my whole life ,and as I looked at him, I knew absolutely that no way on earth was this for me. We talked about Bonnie Blue and Lily Phillips and I was honest and said I didn't look down on those girls at all, but I did think it was heartbreaking.

'Why would you feel sorry for them?' asked Mr. Soulless. 'They're earning loads of money.'

'I would rather stack shelves, be poor and have my self-respect,' I said.

I just needed to get out of that meeting room as quickly as possible. When I left, I sat on the stairs outside and cried.

I was so deflated, and I thought about the lovely life me and Scott used to have and I could not get my head round how I was now going for meetings with the creators of OnlyFans and possibly considering Subs.

I want to be an actress; I want to do amazing things in my career and this would obliterate any chance of that happening. Not only that, I'd be slated all over the media for making such a move.

I can only hope that, for the sake of the children, me and Scott manage to make our peace. I do love him and for a long time, part of me wondered if we'd find our way back to each other.

As far as work goes, I want to concentrate my efforts on acting over the next year and see where it takes me. I'm not sure if a return to *Corrie* is on the cards at all, but I'd be open to it somewhere along the line. I think it could be iconic to see Rosie back in Weatherfield again!

I'd also love to do something like *Waterloo Road*, but I'm totally up for exploring a wide range of acting work. I'm booked to do a play in January 2026 at Bolton's Octagon Theatre, which feels like a perfect first step back into the industry. It's a story about three sisters and I play the one who's an absolute psycho and has an obsession with men – what a stretch, eh?! It seems like the perfect fit and as soon as I read the script I knew I wouldn't find a better home for myself.

So that all feels positive. Despite the knockbacks, every

day I count my blessings because I have so much to look forward to and to be grateful for.

Most of all I want to enjoy a calmer, steadier life with fewer surprises and less drama. One where I can put my energy into the things that really matter.

I'm hopeful.

Maybe the best part is yet to come.

Epilogue

One Last Thing...

WAY BACK AT THE BEGINNING of this book, I said that I hoped that by telling my story with all its many imperfections, I'd be able to help other people. If sharing my life made someone feel less alone, then I'd have done what I'd set out to.

What I didn't realise was quite how much it would help me, too.

Writing it has been emotional, confronting and sometimes completely overwhelming.

This is the most I've ever revealed about myself, and I've been as honest as I possibly can be, this side of getting sued!

But mostly it's been hugely cathartic because it has forced me to sit with and make sense of things I'd been running away from for years. I'm still working it all out and probably will be until the end of my days, but getting it written down has given me a kind of clarity I wasn't expecting.

OCD, ADHD and PMDD (all the Ds, remember?) are always going to be part of me – I'm not looking for a miracle cure. But understanding more about why my brain and my hormones behave in the way they do has been key to my wellbeing recently, and it's helped me stop fighting myself.

This is who I am. This is how it is.

I can't change it, but I can put things in place to make my life a bit easier, to let go of some unrealistic expectations, and to accept that I don't need to be more like everyone else.

Kindness is always a strength, especially when it's directed inward.

I haven't told my story to gain sympathy. I'd never want anyone to get the violins out, because I can't think of anything worse than being self-pitying – that's definitely not me.

But life hasn't always been a bed of roses, and I also hope that I've put right some of the misconceptions about me.

At my core, I'm a down-to-earth northern girl and I've dealt with the curveballs thrown at me as best I can. That's all any of us can do.

If you've read this and recognised something of yourself or felt more seen in some way, then I'm so pleased. That's what this was for.

HEAD & HEART

Life is confusing, complex, mad and beautiful, isn't it? Thank you for letting me share mine with you.

With love,
Helen

Acknowledgements

THERE ARE SO MANY PEOPLE – friends, family and colleagues – who have supported me along the way and in everything I do.

I am forever grateful to every one of them.

To Matilda, Delilah and Charlie, thank you for being my constant inspiration, motivation and strength

To my parents, thank you for being amazing people and the best grandparents in the world to my children.

To my agent Robin Kennedy, thank you for your kindness and for always having my best interests.

To Clare Fitzsimons and everyone at Mirror Books, thank you for believing in my story and for making me a published author.

To Beth Neil, thank you for giving me my voice and for helping me write this book in the way I wanted.

And finally, thank you to everyone who has read this book. Your love and support means everything.

If you have been affected by any of the issues in this book you can find advice and help at:

ocduk.org
ocdaction.org.uk
mind.org.uk
thepmddproject.org
tommys.org
adhduk.co.uk
nhs.uk